Venerable Father

Venerable Father

A Life with Ajahn Chah

Paul Breiter

PARAVIEW
Special Editions

New York

Venerable Father was originally published by
Buddhadhamma Foundation in 1994.

Cover illustration by Ven. Abhinyano Bhikkhu
Author's photo by Lili Breiter
Cover design by smythtype
ISBN: 1-931044-81-3
Library of Congress Catalog Number: 2004109993

Dedicated to Luang Por Sumedho,
who blazed a broad trail to Ajahn Chah's orphanage

Of all the Buddhas of the three times and the ten directions,
The actual embodiment of their wisdom, compassion and power;
Just to think of him dispels our anguish:
Our kind guru

Venerable Ajahn Chah

Foreword

Ajahn Chah lay down his aggregates on January 16, 1992. While I was no great shakes as a monk and have never thought of myself as a writer, I did have the rare and precious opportunity of being close to this great master for several years, serving him, relying on him, receiving his instructions and sometimes translating them, watching him in action, and trying to practice the Buddha's way under his guidance. I hope this brief account will be of interest to those who have read Ajahn Chah's teachings, to those who struggle on the path as I and my fellow monks did, or to those who are simply curious about Buddhism and monastic life. It also tells something of a Thailand which is fast disappearing.

I originally wrote this as an offering to Ajahn Chah and his disciples. This book is not much different from the first draft. I felt it would be better to tell the story in the best way I know how without trying to edit it into literary perfection or spend time thinking up catchy chapter titles. Naturally I could not avoid injecting my views and opinions, but I feel the basic worth of the story lies in the fact that Ajahn Chah was an authentic master whose monasteries follow the pure holy path of discipline and meditation as taught by the Lord

Buddha.

Monks are for the most part ordinary people, and their daily existence is not always free of trivial matters. Those of critical mind and little merit may meditate for a few months or a year and do an excellent job of finding fault, but I feel there's more benefit in pointing out the nobility of this way of life and how it can change people, and the devotion, pure motivation and sheer hard work of these fellows.

I wish to thank the various friends who encouraged me to complete this manuscript and get it printed, including my agent, John White, and also my father, Ms. Evelyn Wechsler, Tom McNamee and Bruce Evans for help in typing and layout, and Ven. Ami Lodro for her cover design. I dedicate this book with the wish that genuine spiritual teachers continue to appear in the world and that sentient beings have faith in and follow their pure advice.

Thai Buddhism is based on the Pali Scriptures, but I have used the Sanskrit versions of some words (e.g. Dharma instead of Dhamma) as they are more familiar to Westerners. A glossary appears at the end of the book.

Quotations at the beginning of each chapter are taken from Lama Gonpo Tsedan Rinpoche's commentary on *Kunzang Lamey Shel Lung*, The Sacred Word of Kunzang Lama. While they are not representative of Ajahn Chah's teaching style, they do indicate the kind of devotion and reliance upon the spiritual teacher which actually can occur in Theravada monastic life.

Introduction

Venerable Ajahn Chah (Subhaddo), also known by the title Chao Khun Bodhinyana Thera, belonged to a tradition of ascetic forest-dwelling monks which has flourished in Northeast Thailand and which was most strongly influenced by Venerable Ajahn Mun (Bhuridatto) (1870-1950). It follows the orthodox practice of Vinaya, monk's discipline, according to Theravada Buddhism. Here I will not attempt an introduction to Theravada ("Word of the Elders") or to Buddhism in general, as most readers will be likely to already have some knowledge of Buddhism, and as there are many books available which explain these vast topics much more clearly and thoroughly than I could. However, relatively little is known about Theravada monastic life, so some background might be helpful.

In this book, almsround or 'pindapat' is mentioned several times. Theravada monks (bhikkhus) were intended by the Lord Buddha to be mendicants, not hermits. Venerable Ajahn Sumedho often pointed out that by having to go to the villages for food every day, and by the monastery always being open to lay visitors, we were forced to present ourselves to the donors, which has the dual purpose of motivating monks to practice to purify their minds and giving the laity a living reminder of the Buddha's way. Monastic rules forbid monks from storing, growing, buying and cooking food, so the monks have to be within walking distance of the laypeople. The monastic community depends on the laity for material support, and the lay community depends on the monastery for spiritual guidance. Monks do not generally go out to do social work, which is something that can be done by lay people. As renunciants they have a unique role in society, and in Thailand this has long been considered the supreme calling. Even the King prostrates himself before a *bhikkhu.*

The method of 'begging' for food is to stand in silence outside of people's homes for a long enough time to determine if the inhabitants will be coming out to offer something left over from the food they have prepared for themselves. In present day Thailand, however, the donors are usually waiting for the monks to arrive with the best they have to offer. Most monasteries also have a kitchen where laypeople, nuns or novices may cook, and often there is a fund to buy food to store in the kitchen. Still, it all depends on the donations of the laypeople, as do the supplies of the other requisites—robe material, dwellings and medicines. Such traditional practices, as well as knowledge of basic Buddhist ideas, are fairly deeply ingrained in Thai society, though it's anyone's guess how long this will last under the onslaught of industrialization.

Many people question why vegetarianism is not stipulated in Theravada Buddhism. Monks rely on alms food, so they eat what they are given. Of course, they are free not to eat the meat which is offered, but purity is seen to lie more in accepting offerings without discriminating as to good and bad than in *what* one eats. The only prohibitions concerning meat are that if a bhikkhu knows or suspects that an animal has been killed specifically for his food, he may not accept it; raw meat and raw fish are proscribed, as are the meats of certain animals, such as horse, dog, snake and elephant.

Some bhikkhus do choose to be vegetarian, though in Thailand this can sometimes mean a lean diet, and some abbots suggest to their lay supporters that it would be more skilful to avoid offering meat to the bhikkhu sangha. Ajahn Sumedho many years ago inspired the Bung Wai supporters to start preparing vegetarian food in the wat.

The teachings of the meditation masters of Northeast Thailand constitute something of an 'oral lineage.' Until recent years, very little was recorded or written down. This is not because of a tradition of secrecy, but because of the simplicity of life in those parts and the simplicity of the teachings themselves; they are not formal expositions according to the texts, but spontaneous outpourings from the masters' experience. In the tropics there is a vivid presence of impermanence in nature. Things grow fast and decay fast: last year's path, if left untended, will by now have disappeared under weeds, grass, and bushes; the simple dwellings don't last long; and the teachings have for the most part been allowed to arise and pass from sight and hearing. Any particular teaching of Ajahn Chah mentioned here is just a small thread in the total fabric of life in his monasteries.

The episodes and teachings I've written about took place in the tranquillity of the forest, where there are few of the concerns that for most people constitute living. Rather than being a laid-back atmosphere, however, it's more like a hothouse. The self-awareness forced onto one by the monastic discipline, and the constant reminder of the teacher's presence and instructions, bring intensity and the immediacy of the Dharma into almost every situation. Dogen Zenji said that by purifying body and mind through austere living, one will gain an intimacy with the teachings of one's master. One evening Ajahn Chah was welcoming a longtime lay supporter who had newly ordained. He was giving one of his informal, rambling talks, recounting experiences, putting Dharma across in personal observations. He talked about travelling tudong, living in the open, walking 40 kilometers a day—"Even soldiers don't walk like that," he said. "It's not that I was strong, but I had energy of spirit ... Some days I'd go pindapat and get nothing but plain rice. I'd think, 'If only I had some salt!' It was interesting to watch my mind while I ate. Who would imagine you could develop wisdom from eating plain rice ... ?"

When some people hear about monastic asceticism, it sounds to them like the extreme of self-mortification which the Buddha rejected with his Middle Way. I myself sometimes felt that we were taking things to extremes, but the kinds of austerities the Buddha practiced and then taught against were far more drastic than anything found in monastic discipline, and they were done not so much to simplify and refine the mind as to weaken the body in order to liberate the spirit from its coarse or evil influences.

A lot more could be said about this, and about many of the concepts touched upon in this small book, but I would like to conclude by pointing out that Ajahn Chah was not a dogmatic teacher. Those who met him were invariably struck by the joyousness which sprang from the inner freedom he had realized—freedom from self-concern and attachment to points of view. One of the things he often said was, "Don't just believe, don't just not believe; find out for yourself, then there will be no doubts or problems, no need to ask others."

Throughout the book, I and most other Western monks are referred to by Pali names. These names are given at the time of ordination, based on the day of the week of one's birth. They have noble meanings, which are not indications of holy states of being, but rather something to live up to. Ordination is "going forth" from the home life and all its trappings, and taking a new name adds to the sense of beginning a new life. Most Thai monks still use their given names in most situations, with the Pali name added on for formal purposes (e.g. Ajahn Chah, Subhaddo).

For those who knew him

I

"If you are interested in the Dharma, a path which is unmistaken, then initially you must find a spiritual master who is fully qualified, possessing all the characteristics and qualities of a supreme guru. You must find such a master and rely upon him intently."

December 1982

If I've ever genuinely loved anyone, it was Ajahn Chah. He's dying now, and it's unlikely that I'll ever see him again; but I'll never forget him, and I think it would be appropriate to make a formal expression of my gratitude. To put it quite simply, he gave me back my life. It's very possible that he was the only person in the world who could have done it. There are a few people who know that this is not an exaggeration.

I think it was November 18. The year was 1970. I had been ordained as a novice in a large Buddhist temple in Bangkok for two months. A dreary grey afternoon in a dreary place in a dreary life. I had just read a dreary letter from a friend at home and was feeling rather depressed (which wasn't anything unusual for me in those days). There were a few other Western prisoners-of-Buddha living in the temple, or *wat* as it's called in Thai, and we usually met in the afternoon to drink coffee and pass time. When I came out of my room someone asked me what I wanted to drink. "Hemlock," I said.

There wasn't any hemlock so I settled for cocoa.

And then someone came into the room and said, "Ajahn Chah is in Bangkok. Do you want to go see him?" We had heard about Ajahn Chah from two enthusiastic American monks who had just been with him for several months, and life in his monastery sounded much more humane and livable than under the other masters we had been told about.

He was staying in a school building. It was a far cry from the plush accommodations that in a few years he wouldn't be able to avoid whenever he came to Bangkok, but at that time he wasn't yet too well known. He and two monks slept under their mosquito nets on mats on the bare floor.

We had an interpreter (Suvijjano Bhikkhu, soon to disrobe to return to his life as Dr. Burns—an independent-minded, scientific, sceptical type, who had checked out several teachers, decided on Ajahn Chah, and summarized a description of his time spent at Wat Bah Pong, Ajahn Chah's monastery, by saying, "Hell, I'm impressed with the guy." He disappeared in the jungle in southern Thailand in 1976), but that hardly mattered to me. I was overwhelmed by his radiant, exuberant happiness. I had really never seen anyone like that. He seemed like a big, happy frog sitting on his lily pad, and I thought, if all you have to do to be like that is sit in the forest for 30 years, it's worth it. So there was hope after all. We newly ordained people had been led to understand that it was necessary to get a foundation of study and meditation, which meant spending a year in a Bangkok temple, before one could go to practice in a forest monastery. Ajahn Chah's words were, you're welcome to come live at my temple any time—if you think you can endure it.

I remember how my spirits were lifted then. In the car going back to the wat I was thinking, there's hope; the practice of meditation and the Buddhist monk's way of life—both of which I found so difficult, much more difficult than anything I had ever done, thought of doing, or heard of anyone else doing—can produce results. Seeing a living example was worth more than reading any number of books.

So, I thought, in a few months I will go there. The terrors of the forest wat were still rather intimidating to think about, so I felt better putting it off to some unspecified time in the future.

But then one night as I sat in meditation, the dogs started howling again and shattered my concentration. The city wat was pretty noisy, so I would wait until things had settled down and monks and temple boys were going to sleep so that I wouldn't be disturbed by laughter, singing, boxing matches, loud conversations, and radios; and around 10 PM I would begin my meditation. But the dogs hadn't gone to sleep. There are dozens of them in every city wat—anonymous people bring them there so that they won't be picked up off the streets and exterminated. Any hour of the night one of them might start barking or howling, and the others would join in. And this time I got very upset and thought, I can't meditate here, I'm going to Wat Bah Pong.

Within a few days I took the overnight train to Ubon. Monks and novices are supposed to sit up on a train and can't take food after noon. The wat I ordained at still kept the Vinaya rules, so that I couldn't carry money to buy soft drinks for myself either. During those 11 hours I thought about a lot of things. I could go to India, live a simple life by the ocean at Goa, eat three meals a day and meditate. But the little voice kept saying, Where will you go? What will you do?

As would usually happen, someone at the train station put me in a taxi for the 6 km ride to the wat. I got there as the monks were starting to get back from pindapat, alms round.

First I met Dr. Burns (still a monk) and Dhammaguto, the English novice who had come with him a few days before. Then the American monk, Sumedho, who had been there for a few years. Sumedho's presence there was one of the "attractions" of Wat Bah Pong. From what we'd heard of him, he was much different from any of the veteran Western bhikkhus we'd met. He had benefited from monk's life, had overcome doubt and hesitation, and had a down to earth approach. In addition, he could speak Thai and was willing to help new people. One of the novices had written to him, and in his reply he described conditions at Wat Bah Pong and the way Ajahn Chah taught, using the monk's way of life as a tool to develop mindfulness: meditation as a way of life. He said that Ajahn Chah welcomed those who really wanted to practice.

After the meal I was given a cottage (*kuti*) in the forest, a simple wood structure with a small porch, raised on pillars as everything is in the countryside. Sumedho helped me carry water for the bathroom, talked with me a little, and invited me to come see him in the evening.

19

The forest was certainly peaceful. It was winter, the weather was pleasant and clear. The sunlight filtering through the trees, the dirt paths, the leaves everywhere: I remember so clearly how it would calm the mind again and again, take me out of my inner turmoil for a while.

There was nothing there, nothing to distract or amuse one, nothing to do, just meditate. The *kuti* was empty, only a mat and pillow, the walls and floor were bare.

In the afternoon the bell rang and everyone went to draw water from a well and carry it on bamboo poles to wherever it was needed in the monastery. Then later I bathed at another well near my kuti.

I went to Sumedho's kuti. He lit a fire outside, made tea, and we sat on his porch with a tiny kerosene lamp and talked. He told me his story and I told him mine.

I had left home one and a half years before to travel and find true happiness. I thought I knew what I needed, and one by one I found out that my ideas were wrong. As months went by and I went from place to place and experience to experience, frustration and despair built up. Across Europe, across Asia, nothing external really seemed to help. Everywhere people basically seemed to be the same. He laughed when I said I found the whole world seething with discontent. Nobody anywhere really seemed to have any certainty. After five months in Nepal I decided to go to Indonesia for one last try. Then back home for a while, and then more travel and then ...? But a series of coincidences, beginning with a case of meningitis just as I was ready to leave Nepal, left me listening to a talk on Buddhism in a temple on my first day in Bangkok. Immediately I knew that this was what I had been looking for, and within a month I was in robes and had a new name—Varapanyo. I had expected to spend three days in Thailand, but it was to stretch into seven years by the time I was ready to cash in my chips.

Sumedho said he had become happy and peaceful through living as a monk. His awareness increased as the years passed, and he only wished to continue living that way. He said, "You won't find a better teacher than Ajahn Chah in Thailand. You might find one as good, but you won't find better." He had looked for faults in the man for two years, and he didn't find any, so he finally gave up. He said, "I really love Ajahn Chah, like a father." He added, "I love my father too—that's filial piety—but my father doesn't have wisdom." He laughed.

And there it was. Sitting up there on the porch in the peace of the forest night, I felt that here was a place beyond the suffering and confusion of the world—the Vietnam war, the meaninglessness of life in America and everywhere else, the pain and desperation of those I had met on the road in Europe and Asia who were so sincerely looking for a better way of life but not finding it. This man, in this place, seemed to have found it, and it seemed entirely possible that others could as well.

Ven. Varapanyo Bhikkhu

Ajahn Chah was away at that time, but the days passed just the same. In the morning, long before dawn, I would walk to the hall (*sala*) for chanting and meditation, wondering how people could live like this, not even a cup of coffee through the whole morning before the meal. In the afternoon I would be dreading the cold bath for at least an hour in advance. After that I would be back in my kuti, all alone with my restless mind. I would think about friends in other places, wondering if there wasn't any other way to peace and happiness, a way that didn't leave a person so exposed and defenseless, and I knew that there wasn't for me, and I consoled myself by thinking, when I'm an old man I'll be glad I did this.

There was a cold spell for a week, and I really suffered with my thin cotton robe. In the morning on pindapat the cold and wind penetrated to the bone. At night in the drafty kuti one or two light blankets weren't nearly enough to enable me to sleep comfortably. And always the thought haunted me, is this what I have to do for the rest of my life?

The food was pretty good at that time of the year, but I was so afraid of letting myself indulge in this one pleasure left to a monk that I would mix everything together in my alms bowl—curries, sweets, rice, fruit, fish—stirring it all together as I'd been told meditation monks do The Thai novices who sat near me could hardly bear to look

Eventually I was to find out what a friendly and good-hearted bunch of people the monks and novices were, but at first I just found them strange and irritating. The strange faces, the smiles, the questions I couldn't understand, the way they'd interrupt when I was talking to Sumedho at the well to ask him what I did before coming to Thailand or something like that. I could speak a few phrases of Thai but not enough to converse.

Dhammaguto and I went to visit Sumedho on some evenings, and after Ajahn Chah came back we saw him a few times, but most nights I would just return to my kuti after chanting and continue with my sitting and walking meditation. One night as I sat inside the kuti I heard noises outside. It was just the wild chickens rustling in the leaves but I convinced myself that it was communist guerrillas (who actually had been active in Northeast Thailand for many years). I sat perfectly still and listened. Instead of going outside for my usual walking meditation, I bolted the door, blew out my candle, and tried not to make any noise. I think I figured it out the next day when I saw the chickens in the forest, but it all seemed very real at the time.

The first time we saw Ajahn Chah there were several monks there, but since we were new arrivals he gave us an audience.

22

Through Suvijjano he gave us instruction on meditation and answered questions. He added that the forest wat was much more conducive to practicing. In the city wat it's like trying to meditate in the marketplace, whereas just by living in the forest half the job is already done. The Buddha was born in the forest, he said: He practiced in the forest, He was enlightened in the forest, He taught in the forest, and He died in the forest. I was to hear that often over the years. One time the following year when I had made yet another request for bhikkhu ordination, he said through Sumedho, "there's no need to hurry; the Buddha died under the trees." As he spoke he was always smiling, laughing, pouring himself another glass of tea, rubbing balm on himself: so full of life, so happy.

One night as we came back from his kuti, Dhammaguto remarked about him, and Sumedho said: "I imagine this is what Gotama must have been like—he's unconcerned." (After I arrived at Wat Bah Pong we heard he was in the South and couldn't return on schedule because of heavy rains, and I had an image of him sitting in a jeep, stuck in the rain somewhere, happy as could be, undaunted by the situation and thoroughly enjoying himself.)

One evening when I visited Sumedho at his kuti he asked me how my practice was going. Well, it was good when I first came to the forest, but lately I had trouble concentrating, various thoughts kept coming up. He told me not to get caught up in evaluating and worrying about things, or else you start thinking, I'm this way, I'm that way, and all of that is just more self. He spoke in ordinary, down to earth language. Ajahn Chah's way, he said, is "por dee, por dee" —find out what's "just right" for you in terms of food, sleep, hours of formal meditation. Don't cling to ideals. There was a man who was an alcoholic who came to the wat frequently. He had been a bhikkhu for six years (it was he who had first brought Sumedho to Wat Bah Pong) and was extremely diligent in the discipline and formal practice; but he was never really observing his own mind, just clinging to an external form, so he never cut through his defilements or developed wisdom, and he ended up disrobing and going downhill quickly. There was another monk, an Indonesian man, who was overly keen on "meditating." Ajahn Chah told him not to even bother doing formal meditation practice, but to work and chant and so forth along with everyone else, and just be aware of himself. He learned to relax and observe himself. I met him in Bangkok later on, and he spoke very highly of Ajahn Chah, Sumedho and Wat Bah Pong.

The practice of concentration was to develop mindfulness, which was vice-versa from what I had heard from other Western monks, who felt that one had to reach a certain high level of concentration before anything could really happen in practice. Sumedho said the practice of constant mindfulness led to a state of balance, and that's what the goal is.

He talked of the way Ajahn Chah had handled him. When he first came he only wanted to sit and meditate, and when he had to do work it made him unhappy. Sometimes when sweeping leaves he would just stand there, broom in hand, thinking unhappily. Once Ajahn Chah saw him and said "Sumedho! Is the suffering in the broom? Is the suffering in the leaves?" He eventually got the point.

Once he decided he didn't like the location of his kuti, he wanted one in a more isolated spot. Ajahn Chah said OK, but there was a catch. He could stay in the one he wanted for the daytime, but at night he'd have to go back and sleep in the original kuti. After a few days of going back and forth he realized that Ajahn Chah was trying to teach him something, to accept things as they are and not create further complications for himself with his desires, which are always changing anyhow. He realized what the real source of the problem was and stayed in his assigned kuti.

I was involved in a similar caper the following winter. It was getting cold, and a monk who was leaving suggested that his kuti might be a bit more comfortable since it was smaller and less drafty. So I moved. But it was near the wall of the wat and the farmers would pass by with their buffaloes in the daytime. This disturbed me because I was still convinced that meditation and noise don't mix, so after a few days I moved back. Someone noticed of course (the CIA has nothing on the monastic grapevine) and duly reported it to Ajahn Chah. He questioned me about it, and over the years I was to hear the story many times, expanded and embellished. He would often use incidents like this (somewhat tailored to fit his purpose) to teach. He would tell people about learning the mind's tricks, how it becomes bored and dissatisfied, always wanting something else: "Take Varapanyo, for example—he came to Wat Bah Pong and was sitting in his kuti, but he wasn't happy. He moved all his things and went to live in the other kuti, but he wasn't happy there either. So he thought, the first kuti was better, and he moved back there. ... " He always told the stories in a very gentle and funny way, everyone would have a good laugh, and he would make his point: it's the mind that does it all; know your mind.

One of the things Ajahn Chah emphasized was endurance ("there's nothing to it, just endurance," he often said), and in speaking of Sumedho, Suvijjano had said, "basically the guy just had guts" and that was the key to his success. Sumedho himself said that illness had been a great teacher, forcing him to cut through doubts and habitual attitudes of fear and self-pity. After his first year at Wat Bah Pong he went off to live by himself on a hilltop in Sakon Nakorn province. His leg got infected and he got a fever. He couldn't walk, so in the daytime the villagers would come and carry him down the hill to another kuti. Sitting there under the tin roof, sweating, with little gnats flying in his eyes and ears, he started feeling sorry for himself, thinking how his mother would be taking care of him if he were at home, bringing him ice cream, etc., and then after being totally lost in self-pity, he thought, here I am, a 34 year old man wanting his mother. He sat up straight and started saying to himself, "Let go," and kept on saying it until he actually did let go. Things were different for him after that.

Sumedho is now Ajahn Sumedho, abbot of a thriving monastic community in England. But he's always been quite a modest fellow, so I hope he won't mind that I'm writing about him like this. I take the liberty because he has been so instrumental in transmitting Ajahn Chah's way—first because his presence inspired so many people to stay at Wat Bah Pong, and later because he was the only one capable of going to the West to teach.

One of the terrors of the forest I had contemplated with dread while still in Bangkok was that of creatures such as snakes and spiders. One morning returning to my kuti after the meal I walked by Sumedho's. He was on the porch, shouting. As I got near he said there was a "beautiful snake," which had jumped off the porch when he came and slithered into the forest, that he wanted me to see.

I soon learned that snakes don't bother you unless you step on them (or corner or provoke them) and I think I did see one or two on that visit. My immediate reaction was calm: oh, there's a snake—they are usually nice to look at—and after that I was never much concerned about them.

After about two and a half weeks it was time for me to return to Bangkok for renewal of my visa. Although life in the forest is much calmer than in the city, it was somewhat of a relief to leave. Often one doesn't really recognize the benefits while there, but after leaving it is seen in perspective. Something opened up for me, and over the following weeks my meditations seemed to improve rapidly. After two months I was finally ready to cut the umbilical cord and go to spend the rest of my days in the forest (or so I thought).

I returned with Dhammaguto. Ajahn Chah was away again and Sumedho had gone to stay at a mountain temple in another district, Wat Tam Saeng Pet, the "Cave of Diamond Light." We were soon sent there. It was a magnificent place, covering several hundred acres, with kutis on the hillside, some in caves, and a huge sala being built on the top. There were only about ten monks and novices. It was very quiet, being 3 kilometers from the nearest villages (alms round was an "invigorating" two to two and a half hour walk).

Group activity and practice were minimal, so we had a lot of time to ourselves. Occasionally I would talk with Sumedho. He constantly spoke of the changeability of things: in one's practice there are peaks of inspiration, and then there are "valleys of despair." I was feeling pretty sure of myself for a while, and when he once said that the desire to disrobe returns periodically, I thought, not for me; I've gotten beyond that. And before long, everything started exploding, falling apart for me.

Since this is intended to be about Ajahn Chah I won't go into too much detail about my own personal story, as fascinating as it may be. Suffice it to say that everything I thought I had developed quickly crumbled, and a seemingly bottomless hole of desperation opened up. Sumedho urged me to see it through; he said I was really getting down to the roots of things, that sometimes all you can do is grit your teeth and endure, and that once it passes, as all things do, you are left with a deep understanding of impermanence that will see you through anything.

Although there was no way out of it, I ran. I went back to Wat

Bah Pong and then to Bangkok.

Ajahn Chah had visited us briefly at Wat Tam Saeng Pet. It was afternoon, we were outside, and he came up to me and looked me over. He felt my ribs and with a very concerned look on his face remarked how skinny I'd gotten—it was not only my mind that had been freaking out. For many months afterwards I remembered that look of concern. In Bangkok things got even worse, to the point where I finally decided that I would go back to the forest and die there, if it came to that, rather than return to the city again. But by the time I had come to that decision, the rains residence (*vassa*, or *pansa* in Thai) had begun, and for a period of three months we had to remain where we were. I counted the days. I was of course terrified of returning, but remembering the way Ajahn Chah looked so compassionately concerned about me gave me a little thread of hope and warmth to hold on to.

The night before I left Wat Bah Pong for Bangkok I went to see him with Satimanto, an American novice who could speak enough Thai to translate for me. Ajahn Chah was sitting alone with a Chinese man from town and his small son. The man looked the picture of domestic happiness and I thought, maybe I could live that way ... ? But one look at Ajahn Chah, sitting above us on his seat, and there was no basis for any kind of comparison: the happiness he knew was so far beyond the joys (and sorrows) of the householder's life.

(In fact, the next evening I was in town well ahead of the train's departure time, and I was taken to the same layman's house to wait. It was not so idyllic—Grandma, wife, and kids sat among heaps of clothes and junk watching a boxing match on TV with the volume turned all the way up. So much for my fantasies about lay life.)

During the pansa Satimanto became very ill and had to disrobe. Meanwhile another young American who had been in the Peace Corps in Africa was passing through Bangkok, "realized that he was a Buddhist," ordained, and was given the name Satimanto. I met him when he came to visit my temple in Bangkok. He was looking for a forest wat and decided to give Wat Bah Pong a try, so we took the train together, the day after pansa ended.

I mention some of these people to give an idea of the steady stream of Westerners passing through the temples of Thailand.

Some ordain, some don't; some stay for a short or long time, some don't ever leave. For every person mentioned here there are a few who go unmentioned. Often these people turn up again a few years after leaving, in Bangkok, at Wat Bah Pong, at Sumedho's place in England, or at Buddhist centers in the US.

As the train neared Warin, the end of the line, the rice paddies, the simple villages, and the monks from Wat Bah Pong on pindapat were a welcome sight. When we got to Wat Bah Pong and went to pay respects to Ajahn Chah, the first thing he said was, "Varapanyo's come back! I thought he was afraid of sticky rice." (*Kao nio*, the glutinous rice which is the staple of the diet in Northeast Thailand, indigestible for some people).

It was the month for *kathina* (*katin* in Thai), the ceremony at which lay people offer robe material to the monks at the end of the rains residence (Wat Bah Pong is one of the few places left where monks still cut, sew and dye their own robes, as well as make all their other equipment, some of it quite intricate. Ajahn Chah has always insisted on preserving this tradition. In most places in Thailand, he once remarked, the only people who still know how to make robes are the Chinese tailors in the marketplace). There are many branch monasteries of Wat Bah Pong, and the monks would travel from one to the other to take part in the ceremonies, visit friends, check out wats they hadn't yet been to. Ajahn Chah got on the circuit too, and Wat Bah Pong became pretty quiet. I spent a lot of time at my kuti, meditating and wondering with trepidation what would become of me. The food got leaner, the weather got colder, and I envisioned a life of walking and sitting meditation, enduring hunger and fatigue, hardly ever talking to anyone.

One cold afternoon as we swept the monastery grounds with the long-handled wooden brooms, I thought how nice it would be, what a simple thing it really was, if we could have a drink of sugary coffee or tea after working like that, to warm the bones and give us a little energy for meditating at night. But, alas, it was like an old friend you know you will never see again (romanticizing the situation always makes it a little easier).

But with Ajahn Chah away, even the occasional evening refreshment was not forthcoming. I had heard that Western monks in the forest tend to get infatuated with sweets, and finally the dam burst. One morning on pindapat, from the moment I walked out of the gate of the wat to the moment I came back in, about an hour and a half, I thought continually about sugar, candy, sweets, pastry, chocolate. Finally I sent a letter to a lay-supporter in Bangkok to send me some palm sugar cakes.* And I waited.

I tell this silly story because it in part led up to the moment when Ajahn Chah took me under his wing. It is also representative of the comedy of errors which was the early part of my monastic career (cf., Suzuki Roshi on "one continual mistake").

Kathina season ended and Ajahn Chah returned. The weeks went by. One day I went to town with a layman to get medicine. We stopped by the post office and my long-awaited package was there. It was huge, and the ants were already at it.

When I got back to the wat, I made the obligatory stop at Ajahn Chah's kuti. He asked about my trip to town, if I'd been able to find the medicine, and finally, what was this box I'd brought back. It was a little embarrassing, as the ants were a pretty clear indication of some extracurricular activity on my part. The various spectators were examining it and concluded that there must be some kind of sweet in it on account of the ants, but not yet having opened it, I just mumbled that it was from a layman in Bangkok.

Then, when I finally escaped to the privacy of my kuti, I opened the box. There were 20-25 pounds of palm and cane sugar cakes. I went wild, stuffing them down until my stomach ached. Then I thought I should share them (since word was more or less out, and I might get myself pretty sick if I kept them all), so I put some aside and took the rest to Ajahn Chah's kuti. He had the bell rung, all the monks and novices came, and everyone enjoyed a rare treat.

That night I ate more with an American monk visiting from Bangkok. And the next night I couldn't control myself. The sugar cakes were devouring me; my blessing started to seem like a curse. So I took the cakes in a plastic bag and decided to go around to monks' kutis and give them away.

---

* The Buddha did allow five "medicinal substances" to be taken after noon: sugar, honey, oil, butter and a substance sometimes interpreted as cheese. They are used as a source of calories rather than for healing. In Thailand sugar is the only one of these which is widely available.

For a start I fell down my stairs and bruised myself nicely. The wooden stairs can get slippery in cold weather, and I wasn't being very mindful in my guilty, distressed state of mind.

The first kuti I went to had a light on inside, but I called and there was no answer. Finally after calling several times and waiting, the monk timidly asked who it was (I didn't yet understand how strong the fear of ghosts is among Thai people). I offered him some sugar, he asked me why I didn't want to keep it for myself, I tried to explain about my defiled state of mind, he took one (it was hard to get them to take too much, as it is considered to be in very bad taste to display one's desires, or anger). I repeated this with others, having little chats along the way.

One monk, Kamun, seemed to be a little older and better educated than the other junior monks. I asked him where his home was, as a way of initiating a conversation with my limited Thai. "My home is here" he said. "If I go to stay in another wat, then that's my home. It's very simple." I asked about his past. He had been a civil servant, married, was living pretty comfortably, but as time went by he began to feel that it was all somewhat meaningless, so he decided to ordain. He'd been in robes for three years and didn't wish to return to lay life.

But the hour grew late, and although I hadn't unloaded all the sugar, I headed back to my kuti. My flashlight batteries were almost dead, so I lit matches to try to have a view of the path—there are lots of poisonous things creeping and crawling around the forest. I ran into some black army ants, and experienced my first fiery sting, which felt like a thorn being pushed into my foot—the warnings about these little critters were not exaggerations. I got back to my kuti feeling very foolish. In the morning I took the rest of the cakes and gave them to a senior monk, who I felt would have the wisdom and self-discipline to be able to handle them. I went to see Ajahn Chah in the afternoon to confess my sins. I felt like it was all over for me, there was no hope left.

He was talking with one old monk. I made the customary three prostrations, sat down, and waited. When he acknowledged me I blurted out, "I'm impure, my mind is soiled, I'm no good...."

He looked very concerned. What is it? he asked. I told him the story.

Naturally, he was amused, and within a few minutes I realized that he had me laughing. I was very lighthearted, the world was no longer about to end; in fact, I had forgotten about my burden. This was one of his most magical gifts. You could feel so burdened and depressed and hopeless, and after being around him for a few minutes it all vanished and you found yourself laughing. Sometimes you only needed to go and sit down at his kuti, be around him as he spoke to others. Even when he was away, I would get a "contact high" of peacefulness as soon as I got near his kuti to clean up or sweep leaves. As I type this I am reminded of the feeling I would get in the city of Varanasi, by the banks of the Ganges, sitting there at night when no people were around, feeling the presence of so many centuries of spirituality.

Then he started questioning me. I had been there for almost 2 months at that point (it was late November of 1971) and perhaps he began to think that I was going to stay for a while. He asked me if I didn't want to disrobe, go back to the world, get married, make money, etc., to all of which I replied in the negative. He seemed interested in why I was there. I told him of my hard time in Bangkok and how I had resolved to come and die in the forest rather than go back there. "Die in the forest!" he repeated laughing (he loved to repeat things people said that he thought were funny and enjoy a laugh).

I had studied Thai while in Bangkok and was able to maintain the conversation; he was very good at talking to us on the level of language (and Dharma) that we could understand.

He said, in the afternoon, when water-hauling is finished, you can come here and clean up. My first reaction was, "He's got a lot of nerve, telling me to come and wait on him!" but apart from being one of my duties, it was a foot in the door, and a privilege. Through it I was to start seeing that there was a way of life in the monastery, rich, structured, and harmonious. And at the center of it all is the teacher, who is someone to be relied upon.

And finally, he asked, why was I so skinny? Immediately one of the monks who was there told him that I took a very small ball of rice at meal time. Did I not like the food? I told him I just couldn't digest much of the sticky rice so I kept cutting down. I had come to accept it as the way it was, thinking I was so greedy that eating less

31

and less was a virtue.

But he was concerned. Did I feel tired? Most of the time I had little strength, I admitted. So he said, I'm going to put you on a special diet for a while, just plain rice gruel and fish sauce to start with. You eat a lot of it and your stomach will stretch out, and then we'll go to boiled rice, and finally to sticky rice. I'm a doctor, he added. (I found out later that he actually was an accomplished herbalist, as well as having knowledge of the various illnesses monks are prone to.) He told me not to push myself too much, if I didn't have the strength I didn't have to carry water, etc.

That was when the magic really began. That was when he was no longer just Ajahn Chah to me; he became *Luang Por,* "Venerable Father."

At first I experienced a great sense of relief to be told that I didn't need to struggle so much, and that I might possibly recover some physical strength. Then the monks and novices began to display a lot of friendliness and helpfulness. The way that they would converse with me made me feel that they were really interested in my existence. It never seemed to trouble them to do something for me, or to show me how to do things. As I came to wait on Ajahn Chah more and more, I spent a lot of time hanging out with the novices, mostly 15-16 year old farm boys, who patiently explained all the fine details of what to do. Their unselfish actions were a strange thing to me. I realized that it probably ran deep in their culture.

There was usually a lot of competition for the honor of waiting on him, but I was allowed to go to his kuti for the early morning chores, before dawn. It meant getting up earlier in the chilly mornings, but I was inspired. The more I hung around him, the safer I felt. He would give me little discourses from time to time, keep checking to see how I was doing, ask me about my past, etc. I began to feel, here is somebody unshakable, like a mountain. "To believe in God is to know that somebody somewhere is not stupid." It really seemed to me that I had found that somebody; he was to me what you always expected your father, family doctor, priest, teacher, Santa Claus and Superman to be, all rolled into one. He would keep on pulling rabbits out of the hat, teachings, things to do, medicines, whatever, so that the situation began to feel open-ended, like there were unlimited possibilities awaiting me, much different from the dreary path I had imagined for so long.

So in the morning I would boil water and bring hot and cold water for him to wash his face. When he came downstairs I would give him the water and kneel there with a towel, while one of the novices took his false teeth to clean them. Usually he would walk around with the towel afterwards, and let me follow, until he finally gave it to me to hang up. His robes would be made ready to put on for pindapat, but first he would check things out at his kuti, throw some rice to the wild chickens, sit down and talk, drink tea. Occasionally a couple of nuns would come at this time to discuss something. It was always interesting to watch the local monks and nuns when they came to see him. They spoke to him with the utmost deference, almost as if they were terrified of him. With us Westerners he was usually the kindly old man, though over the years I was to see him play many different roles. He could make you love him or hate him, feel respect, fear, doubt or disgust for him, and he could juggle your mind states around quite rapidly. For me at that time he was instilling faith. Those early morning scenes were especially effective—the wat was almost empty, most of the monks having left earlier for the other pindapat routes, and we were limited to about 15 minutes before we had to go, so the situation felt intensified—despite the fact that it was so funny to see the great man sitting there with his teeth out, all of a sudden looking like a little old Ukrainian grandmother.

In the afternoons after sweeping his kuti, emptying his spittoon, and so on, I would sit down for a while, to listen as he spoke to whoever was there, sometimes to talk or maybe be given a cup of tea, mostly just to be there. After the guests were gone he took his bath, with a few of us helping him, holding his towel, taking his robe, offering the dry bathing cloth, washing his back and feet, cleaning his sandals. Once he asked me, did you ever bathe your father? It seemed preposterous to me, and I just said, no. Very bad, he said. I had to explain that when we were small our parents bathed us, but we would never even think of bathing them. These differences in culture, education, etc. were pretty amusing sometimes. Once on pindapat an old monk asked me about what I did before coming to Thailand. I told him about my traveling, so he asked, "When you went from America to England did you take the train?"

Occasionally Ajahn Chah too would ask about Western life and customs, about my past experiences, about science (astronomy was usually interesting to them). He was disinterested, in that he obviously wasn't hankering after anything, yet he was very interested because he all of a sudden had on his hands several of these people from a part of the world he knew hardly anything about, and he cared about us.

One thing he never showed any interest in was politics, either domestic or international. Sometime after Nixon was reelected, he one day said "Nixon ran away with it"—a visitor must have told him, and he just passed it on to me with that one line. And then one time when a few of us went to see him, he said "CIA: nobody knows who they are. Who is the CIA? Nobody knows." And that was the extent of the political discussion I can remember having with him.

In mid-December monks and novices throughout Thailand may take examinations in various areas of Buddhist studies, and he usually encouraged the younger ones to do this, though he generally did not encourage much study, especially for the Westerners. We'd been studying all kinds of things for so many years and it hadn't brought us any wisdom or peace of mind, so his advice usually was to store the books away in a box somewhere. He would say, if you have a bachelor's degree, you have suffering on the level of a bachelor; if you have a master's degree you suffer on the level of a master; and if you have a doctorate, you suffer on the level of a doctor. And how could we argue with him? Sometimes I would look at him and think, "That guy acts like he knows everything—and he probably does."

Be that as it may, the time of the exams and the days of study preceding them would be a quiet period in the wat. There was less traffic around his kuti, so I had more direct contact with him. One night after drinking tea with him and one of the senior monks, I told them over a period of two or three hours all about my past, the years of unhappiness which seemed so unalterable, the travel, drugs, school, girlfriends, frustration upon frustration, glimpses of light at the end of the tunnel, more frustration, everything that eventually brought me to Thailand. It really mattered little, and I eventually learned that they generally don't take personal histories nearly as seriously as we do; but at that time it felt so good to be telling him everything, it felt like part of the process of giving my life over into his care.

The months passed and I began to feel that I was really living there at Wat Bah Pong, not merely visiting or putting in time. But before long I was to begin learning how Ajahn Chah trained his disciples. He never really let you get too comfortable. Change was one of the first rules of the way of life. He was always changing the schedule and routine, teaching in different ways, both with the group and with individuals. The schedule might be very relaxed, so that you would start thinking, this is the way it is here, this is pretty nice, and then one night he would give a talk and change everything so that there would be long hours of group practice or work; after a while he might just as suddenly cancel all group practice.

There would be long periods where he didn't give any instruction to the monks, and most of us would feel a real need for it. Then all of a sudden he's giving long talks night after night, keeping us up late, making us sit outside underneath his kuti when it's cold, talking after the meal too, so that I'd begin to dread the sight of him.

His treatment of individuals was just as unpredictable. After my first year with him I started thinking of him as the World's Most Compassionate Sadist. His style was, just when you're getting settled, he pulls the chair out from under your ass. Or, you come in all tired out and ready to take a rest, and he throws cold water over you. I often felt that his methods were drastic and extreme, and maybe he didn't make the absolutely best decision in every particular case, but it didn't really matter, because the practice was to take things as they come, and we could trust that he really cared about us and that ultimately we were guided by his superior wisdom and that of the monk's discipline itself, which contained nothing harmful. What he was trying to accomplish was of itself pretty drastic, i.e. to deliver people from the clutches of *Mara* (the Evil One, the Tempter), which meant struggling against all that was habitual, familiar, and easy, against what most people would probably consider life itself. He constantly reminded us that it was to be expected that we would experience a great deal of friction and discomfort in training our minds; he once said that it was as if we had a friend we had known since childhood: all our lives we had

35

done everything together, and now Buddha comes along and says we have to split up.

But during that first winter I wasn't yet aware of what was to come. The pace in the wat was pretty easy, as it often is in winter, and I had a privileged status. I spent a lot of time at his kuti, went to meals at lay people's homes and took other little trips with him. Then the hot season came. Once again it became very difficult to get through the days, and I started thinking, next year I will go to stay in the Thai temple in England during the hot season (March-April-May), or some temple in Thailand by the ocean. I was feeling very sorry for myself—the tropical heat was unlike anything I had ever experienced. Ajahn Chah was gentle, but he used to joke about me, how I sat around with a towel on my head, brooding and daydreaming. One day he simply asked, are you the only one who's hot? Do other people not feel hot?

Still, the heat was torment, with the fatigue and discomfort it brought me. One afternoon somebody brought iced drinks from town. I drank several glasses, and felt so relieved that I soon started thinking, I could have my family donate an ice machine to Wat Bah Pong, it could be run on the generator a few hours each day and we would always have ice … It seemed like a perfectly valid thought to me. Finally I began to realize, the Buddha lived in the forest and did His ascetic practices without our modern conveniences such as ice, so I could probably endure and survive without it. I later told Ajahn Chah of this episode I had gone through in my mind. It became one of his "teaching stories" about how to contemplate situations to eliminate unnecessary suffering. "Varapanyo was living in the forest, and the hot season came. He was so hot, he was really unhappy, all he could think about was ice. … But then he contemplated, when the Buddha lived in the forest did He have ice? No! He didn't. This was wisdom arising. So then he became happy, his problem was resolved."

II

"Saraha said that if you have found such a supreme Guru, then by relying on him you will receive his oral instructions, and this is just like holding a wish-fulfilling gem in the palm of your hand."

S uzuki Roshi said something like, "our only effort should be to continue our practice." At that period I was immersed in the day to day struggle to survive. New people usually go to the forest with a lot of inspiration and faith, and are able to impose rigid self-discipline for a while, but when they start to lose all of that, it's a sign that they've arrived; all the mental hindrances and obstructions beneath the surface start to emerge. I guess I got progressively sloppier in some ways. But I was still only a novice, and full ordination (*upasampada*) as a bhikkhu was coming soon, for me and two other Westerners. Ajahn Chah had made us wait for many months (by the time I received *upasampada,* I had been a novice for 20 months), but he told us one day that as novices we practiced 50%; as monks we would have to give 100%.

Of course it wasn't merely a matter of going through a ceremony and then having to try harder. The bhikkhu has a very detailed code of discipline for regulating all his behavior, which a novice can only emulate in part, and without the same compulsion, not having taken the vows.

Ajahn Chah also emphasized over and over that we should be prepared to complete five years as a minimum. This was the tradition found in the *Vinaya,* the scriptural rule for monks, but it is rarely adhered to in the present. Basically what he was telling us was that after five years a monk is able to take care of himself; he is literally said to be "beyond dependence." The Buddha, Ajahn Chah said, practiced for five years and endured a lot of suffering; in His sixth year, He found peace.

But time didn't mean much to me then. I really had no future I could conceive of. He might as well have said seven years, or five lifetimes, it all seemed like such an impossibly long stretch, an inconceivably difficult task. There are many rare experiences that one is privilege to by living in a monastery, and living without a future is one of them. That was perhaps the most terrifying thing about ordaining. I have often thought since then that people can sacrifice anything as long as they still have the future to look forward to. To me there was simply nothing else I could imagine myself doing, nowhere else to be, no other life to live. Looking back on those days now it seems like a different lifetime or a memory of a movie I once saw. Ajahn Chah once said to me, years later, "when you look back you have to laugh; when you think what it used to be like for Varapanyo, you have to laugh." The hopelessness and desperation which I constantly lived with seem very precious in retrospect, because I was really living in the present moment. My suffering and difficulty were a concrete, tangible experience that I could always get my teeth into. I only attempted to survive, I didn't fantasize about "getting enlightened" or attaining anything. Later on, friends and relatives would hear about my monastic path and say what a courageous thing that was to do, how it must have taken stamina, faith, high ideals, etc. But that wasn't the case; I was simply desperate. Ajahn Chah's way of pushing people past their limits of endurance was so suitable to one like me. Patience is the easiest of the perfections to practice, I often philosophized, because you don't have to do anything, you just sit there and bear it.

Ordination time approached. The week before, there was an ordination for novices at Wat Bah Pong. During the ceremony I looked over at Ajahn Chah. I thought about the five year commitment. I felt like a groom looking at his bride-to-be and asking himself if she was the right one for him, if he really wanted to go through with it. Yes, I thought; I do.

We were ordained with 19 Thais. Although we were senior to all of them, i.e. had been ordained as novices longer, he ordained us last. This meant that we would always have to sit and walk in line after them. Seniority is a big thing there, and this was one of his favorite techniques, to put you in a position where your pride would get stirred up and wounded. More than merely teaching people, Ajahn Chah trained them, creating a general environment and specific situations where they could learn about themselves (and let go of what they learned). Over the years, he would say things like "of what I teach, you understand maybe 15%"; or "he's been a monk five years, so he understands 5%." A junior monk said in response to the latter "so I must have 1% since I've been here one year" but he said, "No. The first four years, no percent; then the fifth year, you have 5%." So I think his emphasis was on training, not teaching to understand. Which is not to say he didn't teach "profound" Dharma. But often I wouldn't understand something he had taught or said informally, only to have the meaning become clearer upon hearing it again or recalling it at some later time (often much later, i.e. months or years), and this kind of understanding came, I believe, from the training that had taken place in the interval.

As Wat Bah Pong got more well known, monks started coming from all over Thailand to visit or stay. Some of them were quite senior, a few even senior to Ajahn Chah. Such monks are normally accustomed to being treated with deference and respect, but he treated all newcomers pretty much the same. A visitor was told he could stay three nights, during which time he would usually have to sleep in the sala, the main meeting hall. If he was serious about staying to practice, and !;ad a letter from his preceptor or the monastery he came from, he would be given a kuti and put through a probationary period. He would sit at the end of the line and not be allowed to take part in official Sangha functions, such as the fortnightly *uposatha* ceremony, the confession of offenses and recitation of the 227 *Patimokkha* rules. After a few months they would be admitted to regular status, but first had to forfeit all robes and equipment which they had bought themselves. Sometimes they had bought beautiful things which they were quite attached to. He especially liked to give the old men a hard time, the ones who had ordained later in life. I recall one nice old gentleman from a village monastery who had been ordained 15 or 20 years. He had a new alms bowl, and Ajahn Chah took it away from him as soon as he came, gave him an old, small, cheaply made bowl, and put him at the end of the line. Ajahn Chah was not one to humor people's pride, attachments, or eccentricities. Those who could stand up to his testing usually found their stay at Wat Bah Pong worthwhile.

I had been told that being a bhikkhu with the *Vinaya* rules to keep would make a big difference, and just having the third robe to wear over my shoulder actually did make things feel different.

Ajahn Chah told us that as he was our teacher, we were to take dependence with him, and that this meant literally to depend on him for our spiritual and physical needs. We were like children now, he told us—our minds controlled by desire and ignorance, we were unable to take care of ourselves, so we had to have guidance from someone. We were obligated to serve and obey our teacher, and he in turn was responsible for our welfare. This is obviously a radically different approach to living, yet once you're in it, it makes the utmost sense. The same with the Vinaya rules. They cover virtually everything you do in the course of the day, and he taught new monks to take them extremely seriously, to the point of not being able to sleep if you thought you might be violating a rule. Many of the rules mean nothing at all outside of the monastery, yet they are a very efficacious tool for training the mind. Over the years I was to hear him emphasize that the foundation for practice is moral conduct and correct view. The day to day living was mostly unspectacular and often very dull, you might usually feel that you weren't getting anywhere, and then one day, months and years later, you realized that some very big changes had taken place.

He was separating us, the three Westerners (*"farang"*), sending us to branch temples for the rains retreat. Before we went, we decided to talk to him about what we felt was wrong in the wat, mostly concerning the way others were living and practicing. Of course this was in very poor taste, especially by Thai standards, but we were pretty sincere about it. We enumerated the complaints, to which he answered "I don't teach them to do those things" in a very straightforward way. Then he said that it was just the way things are and always have been. When the policeman is around the thieves behave themselves. If he asks "are there any thieves here?" they will say, no, not here. But as soon as he's gone they're at it again. It was like that in Ajahn Mun's wat, it was like that in the Buddha's time; so just watch yourself, don't be concerned with what others do. Then he added, addressing me, "Varapanyo is like a football. Do you know what a football is? Someone kicks it—Boom!—And it flies across the field: then someone else kicks it and it flies off in another direction, then it's kicked again...." We continued talking and I brought up some other doubts that I had. But now he had taken the offensive. "Varapanyo is like a dog with a sore on its head. You know what a sore is? The dog lies down to rest and the flies start eating his sore, so he gets up and runs off to another spot. He settles down but more flies find him and start eating his sore again. He runs away again but the flies will always catch up with him because of the sore."

I was sent to a small, newly established temple in a grubby forest with tiny little trees. There were about 10 monks and novices. Away from friends and the familiar setting of Wat Bah Pong I was once again alone with my thoughts. Naturally, doubts began to arise. I was corresponding with a friend at home, and he wrote to reassure me: "Clad in the yellow robes of a Buddhist monk, you live a life of quiet contemplation, cultivating awareness with each breath." Sounds good. One afternoon during work period, as I hauled logs around in the hot sun, I recalled these words and savored the humor.

Rare indeed is the monk who puts an end to doubt. Perhaps nowhere does the deluded mind display all its subtlety as in the dazzling array of doubts, uncertainties, and objections it puts forth. New monks especially are a prey to it, as almost anything can trigger doubt—doubt about Buddhism, about monk's life, about the teacher, the monastery, the food one eats, about one's ability or "karma," about methods of meditation ... Ajahn Chah and Sumedho both had a very direct approach for getting through the maze, which was simply to understand doubt as doubt and nothing more, see it arise and pass away in the mind like anything else, and not be seduced into following it and building on it. When you see clearly that doubt or anything else has arisen in the mind, you have

41

knowledge: so what is there to doubt about?

Sumedho sometimes suggested the ko-an method of doubting the doubt, but more often he emphasized determination to stick to it, let go of your mind, burn your bridges, step off the cliff. During the hot season before my bhikkhu ordination he came to Bah Pong for a brief visit and I dumped my doubts and frustrations on him. One visiting *farang* monk in particular had told me that the body is the vehicle for practice, if your living situation weakened your body then maybe it wasn't right for you, etc. Sumedho said, "Varapanyo, I've listened to all these farang monks, and they're all full of shit."

But the doubts would always return. With great compassion, Ajahn Chah didn't let people muddle along on the same track forever, but would put them in situations where things could come to a head. So it turned out that he had set me up. As *vassa* began things got quite strict. I felt the noose tightening and I wasn't happy. I was constantly being checked and reprimanded by both the abbot, a crusty old man, and the second monk, a young firebrand who actually did the teaching. There was often plenty of manual labor to do, and the morning and evening practice of meditation and chanting was supplemented by hours of reading and explanation of the Vinaya, which is generally agreed upon as one of the most deadly boring experiences in the great chiliocosm (it even cured my hiccups once). Finally I decided that I shouldn't be living in that wat, and one afternoon I went to the abbot. I'm leaving, I said, I'm going back to Wat Bah Pong. You can't leave, he said; the vassa has already begun, you must wait until it ends. I don't care, I'm leaving. You can't, he insisted. Your Ajahn sent you here, so you stay here. Then I will disrobe, I said, but I can't live here. We went back and forth like this until finally he said, it's time to bathe, and got up and walked away, leaving me sitting there thinking about "going over the wall."

But I stayed. I talked with the second monk, Ajahn Anek. He acknowledged that the living wasn't easy. However, he said, it's pure. This kind of life is faultless, there's no wrongdoing which is involved, no harm brought upon oneself or others.

I sat through the endless readings and discourses with pain in my legs and misery and defiance in my heart. One evening after we had adjourned but were still sitting around in the sala, he asked me how I felt about all of this, and I said that I had my doubts about the value of it. He asked if doubting brought me happiness. What did I have that was worth holding onto? I was just heading towards old age and death like everyone else; what good would it do to remain in ignorance? I said that I thought meditation was the way to find freedom, but I had little time to meditate what with all the work, chanting, and readings. He replied that while I sat in my kuti trying to meditate, my defilements were standing outside, watching me and laughing at me. Learning to live by the Vinaya, the graceful behavior that brought awareness into everything we do, was what could really help me. It was his responsibility to teach the new monks, not to just let them flounder around, he reminded me, and he urged me to hang in there and give it a try. By the end of vassa, he promised, Varapanyo would be a new person. Then he let me know that Luang Por had sent me there for just this purpose. He had told him to watch me closely and not let me do as I please. Varapanyo likes his pleasure and comfort, Ajahn Chah had told him; don't let him have his way.

So that was how the old man worked! One time the following year, when there were a bunch of new farang at Wat Bah Pong, he said to me, "At first just let people be, give them freedom to do as they please; then they show themselves and you get to know all about them. After that you can start training them accordingly. This is the way to teach disciples." Hearing that made clear so much of what had passed.

Once I determined to try harder, the routine started making more sense. The Vinaya began to seem like a golden path leading out of confusion and suffering. I was relearning everything. The rules covered every little action in the course of the day, eating, bathing, walking, talking, dressing. Even clearing my throat in the sala would bring a reprimand—"Varapanyo! That's not beautiful!" Well, from the outside this sounds very oppressive, but in fact it actually makes life simpler and freer. You stop thinking about what you want and how you would prefer to do everything, because there is a way to do it set out for you. And that way is a graceful way, which brightens the mind considerably.

I still had run-ins with the abbot (over the years it turned out that wherever he went, people couldn't get along with him; I just figured we had been husband and wife in a past existence), but it was the second monk who was really the teacher, and he was more understanding. I was encouraged to do the duties of a disciple, such as fold the abbot's robe, wash his feet,* etc. At times when I wished to be several thousand miles away from his abrasive presence, I would humble myself to kneel down and wash his feet. The value of this kind of practice was something I heard Ajahn Sumedho speak about many times over the years. First of all, he pointed out that we paid respect to the ideals represented by the yellow robes, not merely to the individual who happened to be wearing them. By performing the simple actions that the Vinaya required of us, we could lay down the discriminating mind with its habitual faultfinding and judging as to who was or wasn't worthy of respect, and cut through grudges, pride, etc., whereas by just trying to be mindful of and detached from such mental states, one often goes round and round, unable to let go or cut through. And the funny thing was, I usually felt a lot better through performing these tasks, healthy mental states such as friendliness and respect would very naturally appear.

When vassa ended I had intestinal worms and went right back to Wat Bah Pong. Ajahn Chah received me nicely, and arranged rice gruel and a visit to a real doctor. Once I got settled in, I saw that I had grown up some during the past months. Ajahn Chah asked me one day, "You're a little happier now than you were before, aren't you?" He asked what the vassa had been like. I told him that it wasn't easy, but that Ajahn Anek was an excellent disciplinarian. He said that the small wats are good practice situations; you're around the same small group of people all the time, eating, working, meditating, and when you get angry or hot under the collar there's nowhere to go, you can't get away from the people you think are causing you to suffer so you have to look at your mind. I generally found that in those living situations, I would tend to fixate on the smallest things (some of them probably nonexistent) until it got to the point where the guy sitting next to me was responsible for 70-80% of the suffering in the world.

---

* Washing the feet of the senior monk, especially after pindapat, was one of the customary practices expected of a junior monk at Wat Bah Pong and its branch monasteries.

It was kathina season and the beginning of winter again, once more a relaxed time in the monastery. I had more opportunity to be around Ajahn Chah. I think he was pleased that I survived my first vassa as a bhikkhu and was pretty sure that I would be around for a while. One afternoon I went to his kuti to help clean up, and when I sat down he asked me if I knew about *pansakula* cloth. Traditionally it refers to pieces of cloth that people have discarded, especially cloth used to wrap a corpse. Though bhikkhus may not take things which are not offered to them, there are certain exceptions, such as *visasa,* i.e. using something which belongs to a fellow bhikkhu if one is certain that he wouldn't mind, or *pansakula,* cloth which one has carefully considered and found to be discarded. In the present, laypeople sometimes bring pieces of cloth from a corpse and hang them on the branch of a tree in the monastery, to be taken by some monk. Luang Por explained all this to me, then added that "I wouldn't bother doing this with someone who was going to disrobe, but for someone like Varapanyo, who doesn't think about disrobing, I'm glad to," and told me that someone had brought such a cloth. Would I like to go and take it? He said that I should go and look at the cloth and think, this is a piece of cloth that has been discarded, that nobody wants, and therefore it is suitable for a homeless renunciant like myself. Then I should touch the cloth and consider that formerly it was used to wrap a corpse; now I will take it to make a robe to wrap my own body, which will likewise be a corpse someday.

After all this instruction, I walked out to where the cloth was, feeling like the event was somewhat contrived; and the cloth was clean and new. Yet when I actually started doing as Luang Por had said, the concepts came very much alive and penetrated my heart. It's another example of the incredible skillfulness of the monastic conventions, which are often hard to appreciate until you actually put them into practice.

Sumedho had gone to central Thailand, en route to India. There was only one other farang at Wat Bah Pong. A few visitors came. One was Samita, a 35 year old novice, a hyper-neurotic New Yorker. He had been kicking around Thailand and Sri Lanka in robes for a few years and couldn't find a place to settle. I had met him in Bangkok the year before. In Henry Miller's phrase, it was like seeing myself in a cracked mirror. The morning he came I took him to see Ajahn Chah before pindapat. It took Ajahn Chah about three seconds to size him up. He sent his attendant novices away (everything is usually completely public there) and had a nice little chat with us, asking Samita a few questions, through me, about his past and his practice. As we were leaving he asked me what "Samita" means. "The Peaceful One," I told him. He said, "Not 'the Disturbed One'?"

He assigned Samita to me as my "disciple." It was very trying, because his mind couldn't stay on the track for very long, and he would play all kinds of games to get attention, be annoying, test my patience, etc. He was basically sincere and wanted to do good, but he really couldn't control himself. After a week or so I was ready to put an axe in the bald spot on his head.

He did come to Ajahn Chah for instruction, though, and he did seem to respect him. One morning as we returned from the village, walking behind Ajahn Chah, who had a very leisurely pace, Samita asked me to request his permission to go on ahead of him. Ordinarily it was sufficient just to make a gesture of respect and go on, but I asked. Luang Por just gave a half-nod and made one of his belly-sounds, "Eugghh." Samita asked me what he had said, and I explained that we had permission to go ahead. Samita said reverently, "I've heard that is how the great masters answer, they just make a sound like that."

One afternoon at his kuti Samita was asking him about the way he taught meditation; did he use the method of daily interviewing (literally, "examining the mind-state")? Ajahn Chah said, here I teach disciples to examine their own mind-states, to interview themselves. Maybe Varapanyo is angry today, or maybe he has some desire in his mind—I don't know, but he should know. He doesn't have to come and ask me about it.

Of course Ajahn Chah was readily available if you needed to see him, but he definitely urged us to have this kind of self-reliance. Concerning unusual states that might occur in meditation, I think his approach is best summed up by his account of some of his meditative experiences as described in the brief biography of him printed in Thai several years ago. Once when he was living alone he had some experiences unlike anything that had ever happened to him, and he started wondering, what was that?? But then the answer came to him, it was what it was, and his doubt settled, he was able to go deeper into the meditation. Though I should also point out that he did say that it's possible to go astray with such things if one's mindfulness isn't strong, and that a relative beginner needs to rely on a teacher's guidance in such instances. In his own case, he said that when he was just starting out, he couldn't trust his mind, but after a few years he could, and thus he was able to deal with such states by himself.

The end of the year was coming, and both Samita and I had to go to Bangkok to renew our visas, see a dentist, and do other things. Ajahn Chah had been invited to a ceremony at a temple in Ayuthaya, about 100 km from Bangkok, so it was decided that we would go with him, stay there a few days, and go on to Bangkok from there. He suggested that Samita and I might even like to take a few days and walk the last stretch together. At first it sounded good, but I soon had my fill of Samita. So the day before we left, when Ajahn Chah was bathing, I put my palms together in the customary manner of showing respect and said, "Luang Por, once we've gotten to Ayuthaya, I don't want to be responsible for looking after Samita any more."

He turned his gaze on me and gave me one of those penetrating, world-stopping looks. "Varapanyo!" Uh-oh, I thought, I shouldn't have said that; now he's going to tell me off: "I put up with you, so you can certainly put up with him … " But he actually said, "Varapanyo, when we get to Ayuthaya, I want you to tell Samita that he can't come back here. There are enough farang already."

I had never heard of him turning anyone away before because he felt them unfit, and I can only think of one other time he did so in later years, but Samita was certainly a special case. Once we were in Ayuthaya I told him. He was unhappy about it and argued with me endlessly, even though I told him it wasn't my decision. We discussed it with Ajahn Chah, who said that Samita should go to a temple with a routine that he could fit into and submit himself to the abbot there, and then if the abbot were willing to give him a letter of sponsorship after a year of training, he could come back to Wat

Bah Pong.

But after Ajahn Chah went back to Wat Bah Pong, I got more and more exasperated with the guy. Finally we took the train to Bangkok. I mentioned to him that I might call my parents in New York, and he asked if I could have them call his parents to let them know he was well. Of course, I said, just give me the name and phone number. He started writing it down, with a little message. But he kept on writing and writing until he had filled up a whole page and ended with "Love, Stuart." And I was supposed to dictate this to my parents who would be paying $10 per minute for the call! I asked him to streamline it, and then he decided that maybe he would call himself, so I needn't bother. I always remembered that one episode so well because it was a perfect example of how his mind would run away with him.

From Ayuthaya we took the train to Nonthaburi, on the outskirts of Bangkok, and went to stay with Ajahn Sumedho at Wat Pra Sri Mahadhatu. The first thing I said upon arriving was, "This is my disciple, Samita. I'm giving it to you."

Sumedho too was very kind but there was nothing he could do.

Samita went into Bangkok to the wat where he had previously been staying. He came to visit a couple of times. Eventually he drifted away, went to other temples, then disrobed and went home. A few years later we heard that he had gone back to Sri Lanka and ordained again, had another falling out with his preceptor, and went to live alone in the jungle. He was trampled by elephants and his bones were found. When Ajahn Chah was told he said, "Now he can be at peace." Those who had known Samita agreed with that appraisal.

After the New Year I returned to Wat Bah Pong (it was January '73). I was in high spirits from having spent a few weeks with Sumedho before he left for India, and from the rich Bangkok food. The first day I was back, when I went to pay my respects to Ajahn Chah, I told him that I was really going to do it this year, I would master my defilements. This too was well-meant but in poor taste by Thai standards. There were several monks present then, and those words were shoved in my face a few times over the next year when I slacked off, though never by Ajahn Chah—his methods were subtler, and deadlier.

Several Westerners started showing up. I was the only resident farang, and I had become fluent in Thai and the local Lao by then, so Ajahn Chah assigned them to me as my "disciples." He would tell them, this is Ajahn Varapanyo. He is your Ajahn not because he has any wisdom, but because he's the only one who can translate for me and tell you what to do here.

I recognized after a while that being given some responsibility like this was a step forward in my maturation. I also began to feel extremely privileged to be the bearer of his teachings in that way. I could comprehend the language much better than the previous year. I felt closer to the teachings because of my experience there, and I had to pay attention to everything he said and retain it, because the others were depending on me to pass it along to them. Sometimes our small contingent would get a special talk from him and I would translate bit by bit—though when he really warmed to the subject he would half-close his eyes and go on for 5 or 10 minutes before he would stop to let me translate. When he gave a talk to the whole Sangha, I would translate it later that night or the following day. Since his talks could sometimes go on for two or more hours, I started making some notes. I never used a tape recorder, but some of his talks were of such power and beauty that I could practically repeat them verbatim afterwards, such a strong impression did they make on me.

One of the new people had brought Dogen's *Primer of Soto Zen,* containing excerpts from Dogen's talks, always prefaced by "One evening Dogen said ... " "Dogen addressed the monks one evening, saying ... " etc. I began to think, "One evening Chah said ... " and soon I was copying down summaries of talks and conversations under the title "Chah Speaks." It is still in circulation over there, and forms a substantial part of the material in *Still Forest Pool.** When I first returned as a layman, in 1981, to visit the International Forest Monastery, Branch #19 of Wat Bah Pong, established in 1975 for training Western monks, it was quite a feeling when one evening a young bhikkhu ascended the Dharma seat and read the teachings from "Chah Speaks" which had been given so many years before. No matter how many times I read or

* *Still Forest Pool,* Translated and compiled by Jack Kornfield and Paul Breiter, Quest Books, 1985, Wheaton, IL.

hear his teachings, I am always astounded by their simple clarity. I recalled very vividly the situations in which the teachings were given and the young monks who have grown so much since then. And I realized that those days really belonged to the past, because by then Ajahn Chah was "retired" from teaching and was soon to stop speaking altogether due to his illness.

After the fortnightly recitation of the rules, Ajahn Chah would give a talk on the monk's life and the purpose and proper use of the discipline. The themes were familiar, but his treatment of them was usually fresh and lively. This was also when he would give his longest talks, sometimes going on to 3 or even 5 AM. That was mostly just to push the monks a bit, test their endurance, give them a chance to watch their minds. The bell might have been rung at 6 or 7, but by the time the Uposatha ceremony got started it might be 8 or 9. He often kept us sitting there waiting for him as he talked to people at his kuti, took a bath, and strolled leisurely up to the hall. It was over in an hour (unless the monk doing the recitation fell apart; at the first sign of faltering, Ajahn Chah might start pulling on the poor

Venerables Varapanyo and Pabhakaro

guy's robe, crack jokes, or start chanting himself), then for an hour or more he might chat with some of the senior monks, discuss some piece of business (it could take almost an hour to count nine monks to go to a meal at a layman's house). Then he would begin the talk. He could talk without breaking stride for about two hours, but if he kept on after that we knew he was up to something. And he was aware that we knew it, and we knew that he knew that we knew, but we just had to sit there. He would go off on tangents, fish around for things to talk about, ask one of the monks a question and start answering it himself, etc.

As far as I know, Ajahn Chah's approach to Vinaya is quite rare in Thailand. Monasteries which do maintain the rules are in themselves rare, but for the most part the attitude in these places is quite rigid. Ajahn Chah taught that both the Dharma and the Vinaya are conventions, tools for accomplishing a task, and he was flexible and creative in using these tools. So it was easy to find seeming contradictions if you just listened to the words he spoke. Once I asked, you've said that as soon as we've become aware of committing an offence, we should confess it. That's right, he answered. But you've also said, I continued, that just knowing that we've committed an offence is enough, we don't have to immediately run to confess to someone. That's right, he said.

The hot season was quite miserable again that year. I had resigned myself to plodding through, when all of a sudden he changed the schedule. We were to begin at 5 PM with three hours of walking meditation, then chanting, then sitting to 11. Morning practice was 3:30 until dawn, then more sitting after the meal. I could hardly believe it. Well, the senior monks always liked to talk about how tough the practice was in the old days at Bah Pong, when Ajahn Chah was younger and had a small group of monks living under the most austere circumstances: this would be a little taste of it, one said.

Of course I felt very sorry for myself during the month or so that followed, but from the Thai monks, with their ox-like obedience and endurance, not the slightest sign of discomfort or displeasure could be seen. But I began to notice that most of them were falling asleep during the long hours of meditation. Indeed, their bodies being so flexible, they could often sleep in the sitting posture through most of the weekly all night sittings. Several younger monks disrobed at this time as well, and I started to get a much more realistic picture of the Sangha. Even though Wat Bah Pong is an exceptional monastery, many of the monks are there because they are fulfilling their social obligation to spend time in a monastery, because their parents sent them, because they don't want to plough the rice fields all their lives. So I began to wonder, who was Ajahn Chah teaching? Who was it that his precious instructions were directed at? When I had first come to Wat Bah Pong it was very inspiring to see the monks sitting there so silently as they listened to his talks. After a couple of years it became clear that they were mostly a bunch of ordinary Joes whose hearts weren't completely in it. As Ajahn Chah once asked, "Do you really hear the lectures? Or while the teacher is talking is your mind off somewhere thinking 'Man, I really like sweet potatoes'"?

Perhaps not all of Ajahn Chah's monasteries have carried on his living transmission, but the teachings were given freely, for anyone with ears to hear. The new abbot of the Bung Wai International Monastery said, after Ajahn Chah's birthday celebration in 1982, that he always felt that one of the noblest things about Ajahn Chah was that over the years he gave his teachings freely, never finding fault or criticizing those who couldn't practice properly.

Ajahn Chah seemed to be especially fond of those who suffered most. In addition to his great compassion, I suspect it was because he could see the tremendous humor in people and their predicaments, not a callous humor but a real appreciation of human striving. One such long suffering farang was Aranyabho, a young English novice who arrived in early 1973. He had had some good meditation experience as a layman, and he was often positively brilliant in his understanding of Dharma, but he could get kicked around by extremes of emotion. We had many an inspired conversation as we bathed at the well or drank tea at my kuti. One of his most memorable statements was, "Ya know, Varapanyo, what we're tryin' to do is impossible, but we've gotta do it."

Aranyabho had a lot of restless energy, and Luang Por told me he would sometimes see him walking across the wat. "He's probably going to see Varapanyo," Luang Por would think. Then he'd see him walk back, then across again. One of the things that propelled him and caused him to think of disrobing was the letters he got from his mother, pleading with him to come back home, expressing disappointment in him, disowning him, etc. After a few months of this he finally told me about it. Luang Por often suggested that we limit our letter-writing—actually, the original Wat Bah Pong rules stated that the abbot should first read all incoming and outgoing mail, but this was not practical for letters in foreign languages—and in vassa we would refrain from all correspondence. When I told him about Aranyabho's distress and his thoughts of disrobing, Luang Por said "Letters are sense-objects," they move the mind, and this was why he had always tried to control the mail.

Still, I remained impressed with Aranyabho, as I was with most of the newcomers, who all seemed to have so much more clarity and devotion than I could remember myself having when I first came. The ones I praised most highly usually turned out to be the most unstable. Ajahn Chah often chided me for my misjudgments, saying "Before, I would ask Varapanyo, how is the new disciple, and he would say 'very good, very good,' and then the disciple would freak out and run away. Now I ask, how is the new disciple, and Varapanyo doesn't want to say anything. Uncertain, uncertain!"

So Aranyabho decided that he had to disrobe. Since he had only been there a few months, Ajahn Chah let him go pretty easily. He took the train to Bangkok, and a few days later he was back. Couldn't go. But he couldn't resolve his mind. He went to stay at a branch temple and came back to Wat Bah Pong a few weeks later. He told me that every morning he would go to see the abbot to tell him that he wanted to disrobe, and the abbot just said, fine, pack your things and I'll send you to Wat Bah Pong. Then in the evening he would go to tell him that he was staying, to which the abbot also said, fine. Finally he did pack up and come to see Ajahn Chah, but by the time he reached Wat Bah Pong he had changed his mind again. He returned to endure the vassa, and then did disrobe after that. And within two years he was back again, older and wiser. Ajahn Chah really put him through the wringer this time. He told him he wouldn't ordain him until he was 60 years old. He had him wear white and keep eight precepts, as is customary, and would say, you'll wear white for ten years, then you can ordain—as a novice. You can be a novice for about eight years, and then maybe I will ordain you as a monk. Aranyabho sat there quietly as Ajahn Chah would bluster and ridicule him. He waited on him faithfully. One afternoon I visited from Bung Wai monastery. Aranyabho had just taken Ajahn Chah's spittoon to clean. As soon as he brought it back, Ajahn Chah spat a big red mouthful of betel nut into it, handed it back, and said with a straight face, "clean it." When Aranyabho came back again he asked if that had made him angry. Aranyabho replied that it wasn't so bad, in England he had worked in a nursing home cleaning old people's backsides.

Aranyabho became a bhikkhu within a year, but Ajahn Chah kept putting the screws to him. If he asked to go to Bung Wai where all the other Westerners were, he was refused, even though Ajahn Chah urged everyone else to go there. He was sent to the temple in Ayuthaya for the vassa. He seemed to have gotten over his restlessness and was willing to go wherever Ajahn Chah sent him. After vassa he came back to Wat Bah Pong, where I was staying along with a few others. One day I went to Ajahn Chah's kuti and he was there. He had a sheepish grin on his face as Ajahn Chah was good naturedly berating him. As I sat down Ajahn Chah said, "Aranyabho's got dogshit in his pocket." I didn't say anything, waiting for the explanation. "Aranyabho's got dogshit in his pocket. He goes somewhere and sits down but there's a bad smell, so he thinks, hmmm, this place is no good. He gets up and goes somewhere else, but he notices the bad smell again so then he goes somewhere else ... He doesn't realize he's carrying the dogshit around with him wherever he goes ... " There was never any bad feeling when he talked to people like this, because we knew it came from a pure, loving heart; he was offering us, right then and there, a clear and simple solution to our problems, one which he had obviously practiced. His words, and his whole being, simply said, let go—now.

By now, the chances are that anyone who practices Theravada Buddhism will at least have heard Ajahn Chah's name. An English bhikkhu in Sri Lanka told me, "A lot of people here don't like Ajahn Chah, because they say he doesn't know the Dharma." And it's true, Ajahn Chah said years ago that though he once studied all the texts and scriptures, he couldn't remember much of it anymore. I recently listened to a tape of him talking informally with Western monks. "The first level of enlightenment," he said, "Stream Entry— how many things (i.e. fetters) do you get rid of?" Someone said "Three." "Uhh, three … self-view, doubt, and … " "Belief in rites and rituals," someone added. To me, and to many others, this is so refreshing: while some people attach to the words and the concepts, a man who obviously knows Reality forgets the standard ways of describing it. When Ajahn Chah visited the USA in 1979, I eagerly questioned him with my newly acquired "knowledge" of Mahayana Buddhism and its profound teachings. I found that although he had heard or read very little of it before, he comprehended instantly, and he taught me about it, because his understanding of it was infinitely deeper than mine. He surprised me and others by using the exact same similes of other masters, past and present, whom I am sure he never heard of.

In Thailand the various factions love to debate such questions as what is *samatha* (calm) and what is *vipassana* (insight), where does one end and the other begin, etc. Ajahn Chah never played the game. He always said that you can't separate them: when the mind is made calm, that brings clarity: without calm and concentration, how could there be clarity and insight? And in addition, deepening insight brings further tranquility. It's like a single log of wood, he said. One end is samatha, the other end is vipassana. When you pick up the log, you're picking up both ends. Or like a mango, which at first is sour and green, but later becomes sweet and yellow—they are not two different fruits. Without the former condition, the latter would not have come to be. This was the manner in which he resolved the complexities of the scholars and those who clung to systems.

Some things he said, though, might not become clear to one until months or years had passed, either because they were part of an idiom that has to be explained by someone, or because they pointed at something in the mind which you might suddenly discover as you did walking meditation one day, a year after hearing him talk about it. Sometimes he made mysterious pronouncements which I wasn't sure were meant to have meaning or not. Once when he was going away for a few days, he told me and the other farang in residence, "Don't let the dogs shit in the wat. You know what dogs are?" he asked. "Don't let the dogs shit in the wat."

A year or two later I was talking with one of the senior monks, and somehow the phrase came up. He asked, do you know what Luang Por means when he says that? I gave a blank look, and he explained that sometimes when he was away, the monks would neglect their responsibilities, they would form little factions and get involved in disputes. So now when Luang Por goes away he reminds people not to let the dogs shit in the wat.

On another occasion a farang had come back from travelling around Thailand and visiting various temples. He spoke of one monk who had confided to him that at one specific point he became a Stream Enterer, or Sotapanna. Ajahn Chah said, Sotapanna is fish sauce. He looked at me and asked, do you want fish sauce? At the time I was a vegetarian, and to a vegetarian the smell of Thai fish sauce is unappetizing, to say the least. So I answered, fish sauce stinks, not really sure of what we were talking about.

Long after this, I mentioned it to Ajahn Sumedho, and asked him what Ajahn Chah meant by that. Sumedho said that the idea of Stream Entry was just a concept to give people some flavor, like fish sauce.

Again, on his visit to the US in 1979, he related that once a Westerner had come to Wat Bah Pong and asked him if he was an Arhat. Ajahn Chah told him, your question is a question to be answered. I will answer it like this: I am like a tree in the forest. Birds come to the tree, they sit on its branches and eat its fruit. To the birds the fruit may be sweet or sour or whatever. But the tree doesn't know anything about it. The birds say sweet or they say sour—from the tree's point of view this is just the chattering of the birds.

On that same evening we also discussed the relative virtues of the Arhat and the Bodhisattva. He ended our discussion by saying, "Don't be an Arhat. Don't be a Buddha. Don't be anything at all. Being something makes problems. So don't be anything. You don't have to be something, he doesn't have to be something, I don't have to be something ... " He paused, and then said, "Sometimes when I think about it, I don't want to say anything."

As abruptly as it was begun, the period of intensive practice was ended, and we were able to take it easy for the duration of the worst of the hot weather. Once again I hung out with Ajahn Chah. I would usually do morning chores at his kuti and then follow him out on pindapat. One morning he stopped walking, turned around, and looked me right in the eye. There were just the two of us there in the bright morning sunlight: when he looked at you like that there was no place to hide, and panic seized me. A multitude of my sins passed through my mind, and I figured my number was up. Then, in very clear English, he said "Good morning, Mr. Dum." That was the last thing I had expected, and I stood there flat-footed. "Is that correct?" he asked. "I'm studying English."

On a few other occasions we had different types of conversations as we walked. I remember them mostly because his tone was unlike that he normally used, and he addressed me more formally, using "you" rather than my name. I think the first time was when he asked me if I was going to disrobe. I asked if he meant a lifetime commitment, and he gave an affirmative grunt. I said it was hard to think about, that although I had no plans to disrobe, I couldn't really decide that I never would. When I really looked into it, my thoughts seemed meaningless, irrational. He said, "that they are meaningless is the real Dharma."

As rainy season approached he started sending Westerners out to branch temples, to fend for themselves and learn to speak the language. Having been through that the past year, I wasn't so eager to do it again, but all of a sudden I found myself in the doghouse. When I went to his kuti, it was as though he didn't even see me. If there was ice or a drink for the monks, he would wait until I left before passing it out. He was making me glad to be going somewhere else. Years later he recounted these episodes, saying that he felt for me, but that he knew he had to give me a hard time for my own benefit. He would say, now you see the value in such treatment, don't you. I did. He often said jokingly, to me and to the Sangha, "I would be afraid to go to America, because Varapanyo would probably want to get me back for torturing him."

Just before vassa, a newly ordained American showed up. He was just out of the Peace Corps and was planning to stay in robes for a few months before going back home. He wanted to stay at Wat Bah Pong for the vassa, but Ajahn Chah refused. It had nothing to do with the monk personally, rather the fact that Ajahn Chah wanted to put new people through a probationary period, which couldn't be done during the vassa, and that he sometimes was not so keen on people who were not seriously committed but were just dabbling in monkhood.

So the monk stayed a few days and prepared to leave, somewhat disappointed. One night before he left, Ajahn Chah came to the sala to give a talk. After chanting was done, he spoke for an hour with a layman who had come. Then he began his *desana*. He went on and on. And on. After a couple of hours it was obvious he was playing with us. One new monk was foolish enough to ask a question, and he gave a very long answer. Then he asked, does anyone have any more questions? Nobody stirred, I thought, maybe he will let us go now, but he said, "Well, maybe you were uncertain about ... " and went into more explanation. It seemed that he covered everything in the entire Buddhist Canon. Meanwhile, the Peace Corps monk, who had been sitting directly in front of him, was squirming around, changing sitting positions, holding his drawn-up knees (definitely not to be done), and glaring angrily at Ajahn Chah. Finally at 1:15 AM Luang Por looked at the clock and innocently said, "What time is it? Oh, I guess it's time to adjourn."

Perhaps I should mention that we never sat comfortably in chairs, but flat on the floor, and at Wat Bah Pong the floors were concrete or marbly granite. We couldn't stretch our legs out or put our knees up in front of us or use a cushion. If you're accustomed to sitting on chairs, try it for two or three hours and you'll appreciate what it was like: if you are accustomed to sitting on the floor, try four or five hours on a hard floor with no cushion.

The next day the Peace Corps monk came to me to complain. "He shouldn't have done that! What a waste of time! That's the extreme of self-mortification!" (The Buddha's Middle Way means avoiding the extremes of sensual indulgence and self-mortification.) That afternoon Ajahn Chah asked me if the new monk liked his talk the night before. I told him what he had said. He laughed, and said, "I saw. I was observing him. I knew he was angry. Now he won't feel bad about not being able to stay here." Before he left, we had a brief chat. I asked him what he was going to do after he left Thailand. He wasn't too sure. He said he was really upset about something called "Watergate." I asked him what that was, and he explained, but I

58

didn't really follow. It seemed funny that someone who was living the spiritual life would be interested in such things, much less "upset" about them.

Finally the time came for my exile; two days before the vassa began I was sent to one of the branch monasteries. As had happened the year before, I had difficulty keeping the pace. But this time there was no inspiring guidance from any of the senior monks. I remember it mostly as a prolonged dull ache, without clarity or inspiration, but not painful enough to push me past my limits. I muddled along halfheartedly, figuring that after the three months I could return to Wat Bah Pong and somehow things would be better.

We all went there for the kathina ceremony. Ajahn Chah scowled at me and told me I could go back to my Siberia. That's good enough for you, he said. But it all felt so grey. I stayed up that night through the kathina ceremony, went to sleep right after the meal, and missed the ride back as I had hoped to, knowing that this was pretty close to open disobedience.

I slunk around for the next few days, avoiding Ajahn Chah as best as I could. My reputation was at an all-time low, and my spirits weren't much higher. Lots of people were coming and going so I could more or less disappear in the crowd; but when I did talk to someone, they usually gave me flak. Everything was very bleak indeed.

One afternoon I realized that my visa was running out and I would have to go to the Immigration station in Pibun district, near the Lao border. I went to see Ajahn Chah. He looked at me and demanded, "What's going to be?" but I only answered that I had to go take care of my visa.

One of his regular lay supporters from town was there, and Luang Por asked him if he could take me to Pibun. Then he said he was going also. He wanted to go visit a huge forest wat near there where he could usually enjoy some solitude. He sent for one of the senior monks and told him to get packed, saying, "We're going to Laos." Very shortly we were in town. We picked up a few laymen and another vehicle. It seemed that he merely had to show up on the spur of the moment and the people would close up their shops, take leave of their families, and go with him.

He went to Immigration with me, then he went on to Wat Keuan, the huge forest wat, while I returned with the first car. He went to Laos from there and didn't come back for over a month. It was the only vacation he took in all the years I was there, perhaps the only one since he began teaching.

With Luang Por gone and many monks following the kathina ceremonies around, Wat Bah Pong got very quiet. Except for a few villagers who lived nearby, no laypeople came. I kept to myself and practiced as best I could, still feeling pretty guilty about my existence. Every dog's gotta have his day, even in Chah's monastery, I thought rebelliously; but what could I do?

Shortly before Ajahn Chah returned, my sister came to visit me. I didn't know what she had expected, but I explained to her that she would be living with the nuns, and I would visit her when I could. At first I visited daily, in the afternoon. She couldn't touch me or even sit near me, and I had to take an escort with me. Merely going to the nun's quarter at all was quite exceptional, as we never had anything to do with the nuns. I told her that the best way to understand me and what I was doing was for her to live with the nuns, work and meditate, observe what went on around her. After Ajahn Chah came back he cut down on my visits, though she was able to come to his kuti a few times. That was also the coldest winter in 40 years, and when she requested another blanket he refused, saying he didn't want her sleeping too much. After the second request he relented.

She hit it off very well with the nuns, but soon got sick, first with stomach trouble, and then a severe attack of kidney fever which put her in the hospital for a few days. But the nuns, laypeople, and even Ajahn Chah visited her there, and she was very touched by the spirit of the people, thinking it remarkable that they should take such an interest in her. This was how all friends and relatives who came to visit the Western monks were treated.

And life and practice went on as usual at Wat Bah Pong. Ajahn Chah himself was sick with malaria when he returned. In the morning after the meal he would sit and talk with the laypeople who came to see him, telling his jokes, listening to their stories about their families, their business, their trips to Bangkok. Then he would go back to his kuti and spend the rest of the day upstairs, lying under his mosquito net. He said the fever was very intense, but nobody would have guessed anything was wrong while he sat receiving guests. Both he and Ajahn See who had gone to Laos with him were to have recurrences of the malaria over the following years. With him it usually wasn't noticeable, he would just casually mention it when we were sitting around. "Not feeling well. Fever." Malaria? I would ask ("fever" and "malaria" are almost synonymous in the forest). "Uhh" he would answer with a half nod. Once I suggested that he ought to go and get it taken care of. "I'm taking care of it here" he said, meaning he wasn't getting involved with it. Then, not being one to pass up an opportunity, he added, "I'm not a Western monk. I don't have to run to the hospital whenever I'm not feeling well."

When he got over the malaria he really had it in for us. He gave many a long talk, sometimes in the open air underneath his kuti. It was a cold winter, and in the wat there's no way to warm up (monks aren't allowed to light fires to warm themselves). When winter came I usually felt an initial resistance in myself, just wanting to get away from it and be warm, but then my energy would awaken and I would feel quite good. But this winter was colder than the others, and it kept me on edge, gave me a generally insecure feeling. And then when I was getting to feel I could just about cope, he called a meeting and said that everyone had to get out of their kutis, clear a space in the forest, put down a mat and set up their mosquito nets.

I was shattered. This was surely the backbreaking straw. All I could think as I returned to my kuti for my last night indoors was, I want my mother.

So I got a novice to clear a space and set myself up. I put plenty of leaves under the thin straw mat to soften my "bed." We weren't supposed to use any blankets, only our robes, but I decided that was going too far and smuggled a blanket out at night.

The first night out there I was lying down to go to sleep and started thinking about scorpions and centipedes. It would be so easy for one of them to come crawling onto me. They get inside your robe or blanket, then you roll over on them and they sting you ... I sat up and checked around with my flashlight. I lay down again. Then I realized that most of the Thai monks were probably shivering with fear of ghosts as they lay under their nets. Well, there was some point to this after all; take away what makes you comfortable and secure, whatever it is you're familiar with, and things start coming up.

He also started coming to the sala on the observance nights. He was usually too tired out from receiving laypeople all day to come and sit with us at night; or he might come and give a talk, then go back to his kuti. He often spoke of the weekly all night sitting as an important practice, but most of the monks were pretty lax about it outside of the vassa, especially in cold weather. Then one night he showed up to lead the chanting with the laypeople, and after that he started playing tapes, his old talks, talks by Ajahn Buddhadasa from southern Thailand, even a talk that Sumedho gave in English when we went to the chapel at the US Air Force base. When one tape was over he would fiddle around with the machine for a while, then put in another tape. From where he sat he could watch all the monks, so nobody dared leave. He never said a word, and I hoped each tape would be the last—I had gone to visit my sister in the hospital that day, I was exhausted, and I wasn't too keen on the all night sittings anyhow. But by the time he got through amusing himself I had become wide awake and decided to stay up for the rest of the night.

He did that for three weeks in a row, either playing tapes or talking. Each time I had thought beforehand, tonight will be an early night for me, after chanting I'll go back to my kuti and get a decent rest. Then to my dismay he would show up and keep us there until my sleepiness went away. But after that time I got habituated to all-nighters, even used to look forward to them. They produced a clear state of mind, and often a heavy calm on the following day.

One day a nun fell down the well and died. The funeral was on New Year's eve. I had gone to the sala with the rest of the monks for special chanting for the New Year, then just as the coffee was coming around a novice came to take the Western monks over to the nuns' sala. Ajahn Chah was there, the nuns were all there, my sister was there, the corpse was there. It was a bitterly cold, windy night. The coffee had already gone around and an empty kettle sat next to us. I was heartbroken. The nuns chanted, Ajahn Chah spoke, I looked longingly at the kettle, then I looked at the coffin, then at my sister, back to the coffin. I was cold and unhappy, I thought about what I would rather be doing, then I would look at the coffin again. That seemed to be the last word.

We sat there past midnight. Ajahn Chah didn't go to speak to the nuns very often, but the times I was there he gave excellent talks. And a funeral is always an occasion for inspired Dharma talks. Death is not hidden or ignored, and the speakers don't go into oily eulogies about the fine character of the deceased; rather they point out the truth of nature, that whatever is born is subject to decay, illness and death, and therefore one should not waste precious time but rather get down to the business of practicing Dharma. The body is often kept in the sala for many days before the funeral, and the pickling usually hasn't been too professional. The funeral service is a time for contemplation, perhaps all-night meditation or lectures, then the next day everyone gathers to observe the cremation. I usually found these occasions to be powerful experiences, confronting me in my life as a renunciant with a very clear and stark view of the fleeting nature of life, the futility of depending on anything or cherishing fond hopes for something in the future.

When my sister was leaving, Ajahn Chah said he would give a talk to all the Westerners. But when her final night came, the whole Sangha gathered for a talk, and after it was over he got up and went to the village where his mother was lying ill. I thought our special talk had been forgotten, as plans don't necessarily count for anything there, but he told us to wait for him. We sat around and talked, five or six of us and my sister. Fortunately our favorite layman appeared with instant coffee, because we ended up waiting well past midnight. Ajahn Chah finally returned looking very bleary-eyed, but he sat down on his seat and began talking Dharma. At one point I realized that he was all of a sudden wide awake and radiant—that's what usually happened when he had a receptive audience. We went on into the small hours. Thinking to show consideration for my master, I asked if he didn't want to rest. He quickly retorted, "*You* want to rest, right?"

At the end he asked my sister's pardon for anything she had found inappropriate or offensive at Wat Bah Pong. That impressed her very much.

When she left, I knew I was in for a major change. I went to him the next day. Well, what are you going to do? he demanded. I said I didn't know. Wat Bah Pong obviously wasn't the place for me to be at that time, but I didn't know if I could hack it at the branch temples. It was up to him. He said, "This year Varapanyo isn't so happy, right?" I acknowledged that. He went on. "You want to teach your sister, you want to teach your parents; you don't want to teach yourself...." He continued on, and finally said, go to stay with Ajahn Sinuan.

III

"We relate to our parents in this life as having been the most kind to us; and so they have. But the guru is kinder than your parents because, rather than helping you to become established in this world, he will cause you to become aware of negative karma and emotional afflictions you have accumulated in the past, and he will guide you on the path which only results in your liberation from cyclic existence."

A jahn Sinuan was one of Ajahn Chah's senior disciples, though still a young man. His was the fourth branch temple of Wat Bah Pong. It was only about 25 km from Bah Pong, but he rarely left there, so I had seen very little of him. Ajahn Chah said I should go there, Bahn Nong Hy, and tell him, "Luang Por has sent me here. I will check it out, and if it's a suitable place for me I will stay for the vassa." I was to submit myself with the ceremony of taking guidance.

So I cleaned out my kuti and prepared to leave Wat Bah Pong. I felt like I was walking the plank into the unknown again, I couldn't plan on coming back to Wat Bah Pong and Ajahn Chah when the going got tough. I took leave of the Sangha at night, and the next morning after the meal I packed up and headed for the gate. A few monks sitting underneath a kuti saw me, and one of them called out, "Where are you going, Varapanyo?" "Bahn Nong Hy" I answered. "Where's the car?" "I'm walking." That surprised them no little bit. I figured that I sounded braver than I felt.

I walked the 2.4 km down the road, and then turned towards Nong Hy, away from Warin, the nearby town. I kept walking, and before too long one of the pickup trucks that run up and down the road taking passengers for short hops stopped and offered me a ride, as Ajahn Chah had said would happen.

After about 15 km we pulled up at a "truck stop," a few women selling things by the roadside. Somebody bought me a warm, dusty bottle of Pepsi, for which I was extremely grateful. Then we went on. I got off at Nong Hy village and asked where the monastery was. They pointed the way and I walked the 2 km down the "road." From Wat Bah Pong it had been a dirt road, but this was more like an expanded oxen path, tremendous holes and bumps all along the way. I found out later on that they filled in the craters every year, but it would still be impassible for vehicles in the heavy rains.

There was a footpath turning off into a forest which seemed like it should be the location for the wat. I went in and soon saw a few kutis, then the sala, which was just a huge high tin roof on concrete posts, no walls, a dirt floor (one Western monk remarked that it looked like an airplane hangar), and a gigantic brightly colored altar and gaudy Buddha.

"Varapanyo, what are you doing here?" It was Satien, a novice who had been at Amper Det during my first vassa. It was a little reassuring to see a familiar face, even if he was only 15. I told him Luang Por had sent me. He said Ajahn Anek had sent him because he was getting the itch to disrobe—usually the most that can be done when that happens is to move them around, get them away from their home village, and they will hang on for a few more months before disrobing.

He took me to meet Ajahn Sinuan, who greeted me cordially, asked a few questions, then told me we could talk further after the evening practice. I was led to a small kuti made of bamboo with a grass roof.

There were two monks beside Ajahn Sinuan and myself, and four novices. After chanting I took guidance with him and we spoke for a while. He was quite friendly and had a gentle, innocent manner. I mostly remember speaking of astronomy that night— asking where I was from led to distances, geography, the shape of the world (round), and then the solar system and beyond. They were always fascinated to hear about these things.

Morning and evening chanting were scheduled, but he said that since it was so cold and windy we could sit in our kutis in the early morning and just come in at 5 AM to chant before dawn. That seemed sensible to me. He also said that the days before and after the observance days there was no chanting. This was something I had often thought of, what a good idea it would be to have an occasional "day off," but always found that nobody seemed to think in the same rational way that I did—if they did have ideas, they kept them to themselves—but here was someone who could take a step outside of what was ordinarily done. As the days passed I was to appreciate Ajahn Sinuan for having a creative approach to practice and the ability to occasionally employ common sense.

After morning chanting he would always say "put out the mats, take care of your duties," and we would spread out mats over the dirt floor for the lay people to sit on and the food to be placed in front of the Ajahn's seat. Then pindapat and the meal as usual.

I had heard stories about the "cuisine" at Nong Hy: silkworms, bugs, frogs. But it wasn't all that bad, especially compared to some of the other branches of Wat Bah Pong. And the frogs were actually pretty tasty. There was usually enough curry and fresh vegetables to go with the rice.

So I got into the rhythm of life at Wat Nong Hy. In the afternoon we hauled water and then I would go to Ajahn Sinuan's kuti to do chores. We had many good conversations. He felt that Western monks were more serious about practice than the locals and seemed to genuinely respect us.

One day he asked the customary question, do you want to disrobe? I told him that I had never had an easy time of it in robes, and that lately I was wondering if I would be able to continue. He said that all monks go through periods of doubt, that the monk's life isn't easy. It's true that there can be happiness in the worldly life, he said, but it's a happiness that is impermanent and uncertain. Everything is always changing, he reminded me. One day you eat your meal, you eat until you're stuffed full, so that the sight of food is unbearable; the next morning you're back sitting there, and before you start eating the saliva is flowing again. Those simple words stuck with me.

He had a lot of stories to tell about his early days with Ajahn Chah. He had been one of the younger monks then, very eager and naive. He had originally ordained at a village temple, and one day

67

he saw Ajahn Chah walking through with a group of monks. Their restrained, meditative manner was very inspiring. He found out where they were from and went to Wat Bah Pong to meet Ajahn Chah.

A very gruff Ajahn Chah received him. "What are you here for?" Sinuan replied that he wanted to live there and become a meditation monk. "What for? Meditation monks are lazy good-for-nothings, you know." Sinuan said "How can they be lazy? The wat looks well-kept, when I came in I saw how well the grounds were swept...." "It sweeps itself," Ajahn Chah answered.

But Sinuan was allowed to stay. The bell rang in the evening and he came out in all his robes but didn't know what was going to happen. He heard chanting coming from the sala so he went in and sat down. The monks recited the parts of the body, the meditation on impurity. Sinuan was shocked. He thought of the girl in his home village he had had a crush on; could it really be? Did she really have all that gross stuff inside of her? His heart sank.

While he was puzzling over that, the chanting came to an end. He waited, but nothing happened next. Everyone just sat there without moving. Strange ...

He stayed for many years. By his own account he was extremely diligent, but later on I would hear Ajahn Chah make fun of him for his extremes of thinking and acting. He did things like picking up a centipede to let it bite him so he could contemplate pain, or eating food that disagreed with him so he could "let the others see" that he wasn't afraid of illness. Ajahn Chah liked to tell the story of how the grass roof blew off Sinuan's kuti in a storm, so Sinuan decided to practice "non attachment" by not replacing the roof. He got soaked whenever it rained, and the kuti was probably ruined, but Ajahn Chah was dubious about whether or not Sinuan became any wiser or more detached for it.

After a few weeks I went back to Wat Bah Pong with Ajahn Sinuan for Magha Puja, one of the main Buddhist holidays. Ajahn Chah's disciples often convened for these occasions. That year the ceremonies were held at Wat Tam Saeng Pet, but I had an interesting time of it anyhow. We had arrived the night before Magha, and when the Sangha met at Luang Por's kuti there was a big to-do about one of the Western monks who had intentionally violated a major rule of discipline. When Ajahn Chah was told, all he said was, "disrobe; don't want it, disrobe." The monk went back to his kuti and prepared to start walking to Bangkok that night. But after the Sangha had been dismissed, another Westerner went to Ajahn Chah and said that he was concerned about the monk, who seemed overly distraught and not in the right state for going off by himself. Ajahn Chah listened thoughtfully and had us fetch him back. He returned and tried to explain what was bothering him, culminating with an emotional letter he had written to his father. Like many others who had ordained, he found his family unwilling to understand. While his mother wrote heart-wringing letters, his father refused to write at all. This kind of thing was pretty common, and in every single case, if the monk remained at Wat Bah Pong, putting his practice first, the parents eventually came around; after a long silence, which had usually been preceded by several bitter letters, the conciliatory letter arrived: we are very proud of you, we would like to see you, we are coming to visit next year, or, we will be happy to pay your plane fare any time you want to come visit. (Ajahn Sumedho said that when he first received such a letter, his father had added "P.S.—please don't come home naked," so he though that maybe his father still had some lingering misconceptions about monastic life). Without exception this is how it turned out for those who stuck to it and didn't let themselves get bowled over by sentiment.

This was to eventually happen with this monk also, but not just yet. He had always been very independent-minded, occasionally refusing to comply with Ajahn Chah's wishes, and he seemed to suffer for it in various ways. Now he was describing how he had tried to communicate with his father over the years, but to no avail. In tears, he tried to tell Ajahn Chah in somewhat garbled Thai what he had written in his last letter, ending with "I am your son; are you my father?"

Ajahn Chah seemed sympathetic to what he was going through, and told him to stay for a while. He would eventually have to go to another temple to do probation and penance for his breach of discipline, but Ajahn Chah wanted him to stay around, calm down first, take it easy. In the two years he had been a bhikkhu he had practiced very hard, maintaining a rigid manner of external discipline. It was falling apart now, and what was inside was surfacing. Luang Por wanted him to relax a little; as I heard him and Ajahn Sumedho say so many times, just to go on pindapat, eat his meal, sweep the leaves, etc., without striving, without concern.

I inadvertently seemed to cash in on this monk's misfortune. For months I had been in Chah's doghouse, while hearing him extolled as the model of diligence and endurance. All of a sudden he took my place in the doghouse, and I even heard myself praised by my Ajahn for being able to hang in there without going to such extremes. The night after Magha, Ajahn Chah was back from Tam Saeng Pet, talking with a few monks at his kuti. They discussed this monk, and Luang Por did an imitation of him, rubbing his eyes and crying, "He's my father, I'm his son ... " He laughed and shook his head. To him, this kind of psychotherapeutic drama just seemed to be a lot of pathetic confusion. I remember it very distinctly, as an example of the way he saw through the self-important attitude that Westerners are especially prone to, how it needlessly glorifies, and increases, suffering.

There were two Western laymen visiting then. They had been there for a few days and were having some difficulty with the food. They mentioned it to Ajahn Chah. They said that if they ate enough of the glutinous rice to keep from being hungry later in the day, they just felt heavy and uncomfortable. So they had been eating smaller amounts, but now felt hungry in the evening, which made them think about food, distracted them from meditation, etc. They suggested that it would be better if they could eat some fruit in the afternoon to balance things out and help their meditation. Ajahn Chah listened as Sumedho translated all this to him, then he said, "When you come here to practice with Sumedho, you should get to know how Sumedho lives. He eats one meal a day, and sometimes he's hungry at night. It's better for you to experience this, then you can understand his practice. For example, sometimes Sumedho sits in meditation (doing the meditation on the parts of the body): "hair of the head ... bodily hair ... nails ... teeth ... skin ... coffee. ... "

Later that night I had an enthusiastic conversation with Sumedho. My spirits were reviving, and I proclaimed to him, "If I make it through this hot season, nothing can stop me." Stop me from doing what? From surviving, I guess. For many of us it was enough of a task just to be able to continue as monks with Ajahn Chah.

The next morning I went to take leave of him. He was talking with some lay people. I did my prostrations to him and remained kneeling rather than sitting down, hoping to indicate that I just needed a brief moment of his attention. He turned to look at me, I begged to take leave, and he just said "Don't come back" with a lovely warm smile. Sixth month, full moon, I said, meaning the Visakha Puja celebration, three months later.

So it was back to Nong Hy for the long haul. It certainly wasn't a comfortable life, but I liked Ajahn Sinuan and felt that I could probably manage, which was a lot more positive than the way I'd felt about my stays in the other branch temples.

My practice became pretty regular, mostly for want of distractions. No lay people ever came driving in to look around or to visit Ajahn Sinuan, the food was always pretty much the same, I had no friends to hang out with and kill time, and Ajahn Sinuan didn't retain us for long talks after evening chanting as Ajahn Chah often did.

Now when I think back on those days I tend to recall the highlights of inspiration, humor, or difficulty, but in actuality there was a constant intensity and challenge in the daily living. Every day seemed significant at the time, and no time was wasted. Working, eating, bathing at the well, trying to apply mindfulness, it was all part of the job of being a monk, and I pretty much felt like I was on the job all the time.

That was also when I realized that I probably would actually make the five years. I even began thinking, only 31 months left until the end of my fifth vassa.

Things remained quiet in the wat, only six or eight of us (on about 50 acres). The winter extended itself an extra month, and the heat wasn't too bad when it did come. Ajahn Sinuan seemed to be quite a good teacher, both in the pointers he gave us and in the talks he gave to the lay people. I was sometimes actually astounded at the profundity of some of his talks to the very small group of people who came to spend the night on observance days. And he would often suggest skillful ways to sharpen awareness or points to recollect, which seemed to come from his own experience.

71

Once I asked him about the practice of the lay people. He told me that the only thing they came for was to get lottery numbers. They would spend the whole night at the wat in order to glean some numbers from the talk; they were all convinced that the meditation monks had the power to see the winning numbers, and that they gave them out in subtle ways. If the Ajahn talked about the Four Noble Truths and the Eightfold Path, they would derive 48, or add

Varapanyo Bhikkhu at his kuti at Wat Nong Hy

the digits to get 12, or multiply them ... Sinuan was convinced that every layperson who came to the monastery was like that. I don't think it was quite that bad, but there were some who came only for a number, as I was to see when we farang had our own wat at Bung Wai later on, and there were a lot of regulars who came out of devotion but also believed that we did have the numbers to give. When Sumedho became abbot at Bung Wai he mentioned the silliness and impropriety of this custom in his lectures to the lay people in no uncertain terms, and occasionally came down quite hard on those who came only for a number and got pushy or obnoxious about it. When I visited in 1982, I took a taxi from town to the wat one day, and the driver mentioned Ajahn Sumedho (who had gone to England years before). He indicated his high regard for Ajahn Sumedho, and I agreed with him. "He really gave good numbers," he said. "Correct every time." I replied that Ajahn Sumedho never gave lottery numbers, but he was certain of it. "Oh sure, he sat up there and gave out the numbers when he spoke ..." I realized there was no way to convince him otherwise.

Ajahn Chah himself didn't seem to be bothered by that too much, but he was discouraged with the general level of interest Thai people had in Dharma. He often said that he felt like a monkey on a string. People came to look at him, poked him to watch him jump around; "when I get tired maybe they throw me a banana." Especially after his trips to America and England, he spoke about Buddhism dying out in Thailand; he saw that it was different in the West.

I got along well with Ajahn Sinuan but I had to learn that he too had his quirks. Part of it was his heritage, I think. The people in the Nong Hy area were of a particular ethnic group, called Soey, who were generally considered primitives. Luang Por would slyly ask me, "When you went to the villages there, were they clean?" Or "Are the people in Nong Hy nice-looking?" Ajahn Sinuan once mentioned that Sumedho had told him that in America there are machines that sell you a Pepsi, and that when you go to a store to buy things they add everything up on a machine. He was particularly intrigued that the Pepsi machines could even give change. "How does the machine know?" he would ask.

He also had a stubborn streak which later led to a few heated discussions. He had a peculiar way of reasoning that many people found exasperating. We would often sweep the grounds for 2-3 hours in the afternoon, and for our evening refreshment he would send a novice around to the kutis to give everyone two small sucking candies. Somehow he always seemed to have a supply of them. It turned out that he sent a layman to town to buy them, along with sugar, cocoa, and tea. But he was reluctant to let us have sweet drinks because "once you use these things, then you don't have them anymore." This was a big issue to me, of course, but his reasoning extended to much weightier things as well. Later on I was to hear how he built many kutis that collapsed. He believed that complicated plans and methods weren't necessary; you just needed to use common sense. When you sunk the pillars, they didn't have to be set in concrete, but could be set right in the earth. So his kutis fell down, his water tank burst. When confronted, he would pull rank. One monk told me that he was at Nong Hy when Ajahn Sinuan first went there to establish the wat. In clearing the forest, Sinuan had the large trees cut down and left the small ones. The monk asked, "Ajahn, wouldn't it be better to leave the big trees for shade?" Sinuan's answer was, "Don't argue with the Ajahn." The monk said they spent some very uncomfortable hot seasons with no shade for the kutis. Then when they were building toilets, Sinuan insisted on putting them upwind of the sala. The monk pointed out the error; again, "Don't argue with the Ajahn." So the toilets were built upwind of the sala, and "the lay people all ran away."

Like many monks, Sinuan was obsessed with his stomach. He said that he had ulcers, and as a result he didn't like to do the all night sittings, otherwise his ulcers would flare up and he couldn't perform his functions as abbot. He said that Ajahn Chah criticized him for this. He felt that the old man had it in for him. He said, "I don't know what Luang Por wants from me. Luang Por has said, 'If Sinuan is suffering, I'm happy; when Sinuan is suffering, I raise my hands and "wai" (anjali, the gesture of respect or approval).'"

On one of my visits to Wat Bah Pong, Ajahn Chah innocently asked, "Varapanyo! At Wat Nong Hy do you do the all night sittings?" I replied that I tried to stay up, or perhaps sleep only an hour or two. "Does Ajahn Sinuan stay up all night?" Not usually, no. "Have you *ever* seen Ajahn Sinuan stay up all night?" No, I hadn't. I gave him Sinuan's explanation, which he had doubtless heard before. Then he said, "When you go back to Nong Hy, I want you to take a message to Ajahn Sinuan. Tell him, Luang Por says he should sit up all night from now on ... even if he has to die."

When I was back in the Frog Pond, as I had come to think of it, Sinuan eventually asked if Luang Por had sent any messages. We were walking to the village for pindapat. He didn't like what he heard, and he really started carrying on. "I take refuge in the

Buddha, the Dharma, and the Sangha: Buddham Saranam Gacchami* ... I don't say Luang Por Saranam Gacchami ... What does Luang Por do anyhow? Does *he* stay up all night ... ?" I was rather scandalized to hear such talk (though perhaps it was another tribute to Luang Por's skill at poking in the right spot), especially in front of the newly ordained novices who were with us. For a long time it had been understood that Ajahn Chah was the teacher of all those living in the various branch monasteries of Wat Bah Pong, and he was always spoken of in the most respectful manner.

Back in the wat I was upset. After the meal the discussion began again, and I took the offensive. I said that we should try to follow our teacher's instructions, and not bad-mouth him in front of others. Sinuan's second monk came to his defense, reminding me of his health problem. Then he said, if you feel that way, why don't you join in the afternoon work? Most of the afternoon was devoted to heavy labor. That often happens during the vassa. Although it is supposed to be a period devoted to formal meditation practice, the Ajahns usually prefer to keep the temporarily ordained monks busy with work. Sinuan had excused me from work to do my own practice, partly because I wasn't as strong as those farm boys. We debated this, and the monk said he would like to see with his own eyes if I wasn't strong enough to haul bricks.

So the wheelbarrow was loaded up for me, I took off my upper robe, and went to it. I tried to push the barrow up the slope, but only got part way. I tried a few times and then gave up, soaked with sweat. It was very funny to everyone except me.

After the vassa when I was back at Bah Pong, Luang Por asked me if I had given Ajahn Sinuan his message. I described the whole incident for him. He laughed. "Varapanyo put his Ajahn to task." Then he said, "OK. New instructions. Next time you go to Nong Hy, tell Ajahn Sinuan he should take it easy from now on ... eat two meals a day ... get lots of rest. He's an old man (he was 35); he must be about 70 now, right?"

We had several spirited run-ins, and I acted in ways that most Thais would have choked over, but Sinuan kept his sense of humor

---

* The traditional Pali phrase for expressing devotion to the Triple Gem of Buddha, Dhamma, Sangha, meaning literally, "I go to the Buddha for refuge," etc.

and perspective. When vassa was approaching he took in a large number of local boys for temporary ordination, most of them novice age. They were a wild bunch. To my horror I found myself listening to discourses and readings two or three times a day. Sinuan would sit there telling his buffalo jokes (e.g. "being born human is a special opportunity—if you got a buffalo to sit cross-legged to meditate he'd shit all over himself") and enjoying himself immensely, while I fumed and wished him fiery ulcers. I knew it was a chance for me to let go, but I thought to myself, I can't give him the satisfaction of having helped me.

Then when the meetings were over, they would go back to their kutis, open their chanting books, and start wailing. I guess it was the only way they could really pass the time, but it was distracting. Sinuan and I discussed it several times, and he occasionally suggested that they chant softly so as not to disturb others who were meditating, but to little avail.

So one morning I entered the sala during morning sitting chanting in a loud voice. Nobody stirred. I took my seat. We went through the morning routine, while I wondered if I'd gone too far. After the meal Sinuan said something about being considerate of others: "Did you hear the farang this morning?"—And he imitated me in a nasal voice, laughing—"he's trying to ask you to chant softly when you practice in your kuti."

One morning after the all night sitting I was lying down to sleep in my kuti, and just as I drifted off the novices started laughing and playing at the well, which was nearby. I popped up off the floor, wide awake. I spent the next few hours trying to get back to sleep, without success. I tried again after the afternoon chores, then walked around the wat on rubbery legs trying to calm down. I took a bath, went to my kuti, and started sitting cross-legged. As soon as I got calm, the howls came from the well. I was shattered. I thought, I'll just lie down until it gets dark, then no one else will be coming to the well, and I will sit again. I did, and once again as I was getting settled, somebody started chanting, loud. That did it for me. Still in the cross-legged posture, I screamed at the top of my lungs, in English, "QUIET!"

The chanting stopped. Someone else nearby called out to the chanting monk. "Hey, I think maybe you should chant softly."

A minute later several monks and novices were at my kuti. Ajahn Som, the second monk, asked worriedly what was wrong. I muttered, I can't handle it any more, I can't compete with them, I can't handle it … Then Sinuan came, and I explained my frustration. He seemed to understand. He laughed and said, "I thought someone had slit your throat." Then as he was leaving, he said "Next time you should consult me first."

During that vassa my parents came to visit. I went to Wat Bah Pong to receive them there. Like the parents of other monks who came, they were reassured by what they saw and heard, and much impressed with Ajahn Chah and Sumedho. I always felt that the quality of life at Wat Bah Pong must have been very tangible to these people. Indeed, even Thai city people were often immediately struck by the tranquil orderliness of the forest wat when they came for the first time. Sumedho was able to explain what it was about in ways they could understand, and Ajahn Chah charmed them right out of themselves. "There's something about him," my mother had to admit.

Still, after they had been there about a week, I began to worry that they perhaps didn't really understand as much as they should. One night I went to Luang Por and told him of my concern. He said, "You've been here three years; do you understand everything yet?" I had to admit that I didn't. Little by little, he said; no need to worry about it. He turned to a layman who was there and said, "He's worried about his parents … My mother's in the box up there." He laughed (his ancient mother had finally expired and her body was being kept in the sala in preparation for a grand funeral).

My parents went to Nong Hy twice, and on the second occasion my father spent the night. We had a friendly, meaningful talk with Ajahn Sinuan. In the morning he walked to the village with us and partook of the meal. When I asked him how he liked the food, he said, "The frog was good, but the bamboo shoots were a little spicy."

Varapanyo Bhikkhu, Ajahn Sinuan, and some of the novices, with Varapanyo's father at Wat Nong Hy.

IV

*"The Buddha appeared in the past; but without the Guru to be
your friend and guide in the present, you wouldn't really follow
the Buddha's teachings; you wouldn't be so motivated and you
wouldn't know how to practice them properly. So in this way the
Guru is far kinder to you than the Buddha was."*

(May, 1986)

It was 1974, and I was still down in the Frog Pond with Ajahn
(who is now Mr.) Sinuan. That was the year that Ajahn Chah
instituted his annual birthday gathering, where the Sangha
would come together to "tam wat"* him, rather than coming in
small groups after the vassa had begun, and where there would be
a Sangha meeting. I had come to Wat Bah Pong in May, as I vaguely
recalled Luang Por having said something about training the farang
monks at Visakha time, though when I arrived he was gone and
nobody knew anything about it; still, it was an excuse for a
"vacation." I went to the much-feared dentist at the Ubon hospital,
and decided to wait around for the birthday party, after which I could
return to Nong Hy with Ajahn Sinuan.

At the Sangha meeting, Luang Por asked if anyone had anything
to discuss. As could be expected, nobody said anything—until
Sinuan spoke up. It was a disgrace, he said, the way monks,
especially the senior Ajahns, were always falling asleep during
desanas and all-night sittings. This was one of his pet peeves. I had
often heard him expound on this, and heard him boast that nobody

---

* A formal ceremony of respect for a senior monk or teacher, traditionally
performed before or during the vassa.

ever saw *him* falling asleep (though nobody ever saw him trying to sit up all night, either). Ajahn Chah acknowledged this, but didn't have much to say about it. In past years we brash farang had brought up the subject of poor posture in meditation, and why didn't people receive training in how to sit. Luang Por's answer then had been, "What's so difficult about sitting properly, just do this," as he sat beautifully erect without strain or slackness. Then he said, "Have you ever seen any monks falling asleep behind their bowls at meal time? No, they're like this"—and he imitated someone sitting ramrod upright, bright-eyed and alert. "It has to have food," he said good-naturedly, as many Thai monks seethed (I found out later) at this latest farang indiscretion.

Then (in the Sangha meeting) Luang Por brought up a few items. Prostrations. It gets worse all the time, he said. "Sinuan's stopped prostrating altogether" he said in terse Lao, and he did an imitation, bending his head slightly and fluttering his hands, as the city ladies usually do.

Back at Nong Hy a few days later, I was at Sinuan's kuti one afternoon, and he said, "I really told them, didn't I?" i.e. about the Ajahns falling asleep. I replied, "Luang Por really told you, didn't he?" i.e. about prostrating. He saw red. Changing to his I'm-right-and-nobody-can-tell-me-anything tone, he said that prostrations are only a convention, it doesn't matter what you do externally, it's what's in your mind that's important, etc. I said if that's the case, then I can sit like this—and leaning back on one elbow, I stuck both feet out at him. Fortunately there was nobody else there to see this. Probably any other Thai Ajahn would have been stunned right out of his skirt, but Sinuan (whom another Jewish monk and I had decided must have been our mother-in-law in a past life) didn't bat an eyelash, though when our relationship was strained to breaking later on he brought this up and said that anyone else would have kicked me out of their wat.

So life went on. When it became obvious that I was in for another vassa of work and Vinaya readings, I threatened to leave a couple of times, even packing my gear and cleaning out my kuti once. But he was patient and kind, even finally allowing me to practice in my kuti during some of these group activities.

As I mentioned, there were a large number of temporary

ordinations, especially novices. They were pretty wild kids, and Sinuan did little to control, and often much to encourage, them, such as playing games with the dogs (feeding them while we were eating, making sunglasses for them out of cardboard and colored plastic wrapping paper). One day I confronted him about one boy. How can you just let him run wild in your monastery? I asked. He countered by offering me the chance to train the boy. So we tried. It turned out that Narong had been something of a juvenile delinquent in the village, but I liked him and felt that he needed some attention. He would boil water for me, I would give him a little instruction and chores to do. It seemed to be working, and I became inspired with utopian visions of new ways of education. Then we had a falling out, he wouldn't listen to me anymore. I took him to see Sinuan. I aired my complaints. Sinuan asked Narong, who was by now in tears, if he wished to continue with me. The answer was no. Sinuan said, "You see, it's not so easy." It was a good lesson, and one that another Ajahn wouldn't have been inventive enough to give.

But by the time the end of the vassa approached I'd had enough. I felt inclined to seek out some serious training and group practice, perhaps with Ajahn Jun, Luang Por's second senior-most disciple. Two days after vassa we went to the kathina at Wat Bah Pong. There wasn't going to be a kathina at Nong Hy, so I took my leave of Ajahn Sinuan. I had long since gotten out of Luang Por's doghouse, and was basking in the afterglow of having recited the Patimokkha during my parent's visit in the vassa, when I surprised Luang Por and the whole Sangha by finally doing something well. So Luang Por received me as just another monk, and I could feel that internally and externally things were on a new footing. It seemed like a turning point. One afternoon, alone with him at his kuti, Luang Por asked me if I was going to disrobe. It was one of those rare conversations where he spoke to me in a serious and direct way, and therefore that sticks out in my memory. I asked if he meant, was I going to be a monk for the rest of my life? That's what I meant, he said. I told him that I couldn't make my mind agree on it, but added, I've got faith to persevere. He acknowledged this by saying, "It's better than before, isn't it?"

"Will you disrobe?" is a common question, and one that he

81

certainly took seriously, but once when I told him that in moments of inspiration I thought, I won't just ordain for all of this life, but for ten lives in the future, he just remarked "Oh, ten lives of misery, huh?"

The time after vassa is usually a more relaxed time in the wat, but I didn't particularly feel like I could relax. I could see a little beyond merely surviving and look more clearly at the immediacy of birth and death and the terrors of endless samsara. There was something spurring me. While it kept me from being too slack, I think it made it impossible to relax and to appreciate subtler aspects of Dharma, Vinaya, and Ajahn Chah himself. But it seems like that's the way the training has to go, experiencing extremes until one finds the middle. Luang Por compared it to a child learning to write, the letters come out crooked and sloppy, and the only thing to do is keep practicing.

In early December we went to a Pah Bah ceremony at Wat Bah Klor, a new temple in Amper Det Udom. About a hundred people filled the small sala. After Luang Por went back to Wat Bah Pong, I stayed on with a few others. A few lay people would come in the morning, five or six would spend the night on Wan Pra. It made me realize how wherever Ajahn Chah went, people would turn out in such large numbers.

End of the year was visa time, so I went back to Wat Bah Pong. Work had begun clearing the land for the Uposatha hall (chapel, or *"bote"*). Most wats in Thailand are eager to build a bote, whether they have any use for it or not, and they all come out looking the same. Luang Por had resisted the urging of his lay followers for a long time, but now that he'd decided to do it he seemed to be quite taken up with it; some farang monks even started asking, do you think Luang Por has a "bote kilesa"?* The design seemed to be known only to him, and the final result was quite magnificent, unlike anything I've seen anywhere else in Thailand (except some of the banks in Bangkok, perhaps). He had become an *upajjhaya*, or preceptor, by this time, and having a bote would make Wat Bah

---

* *Kilesa* = mental defilement. The word was used in casual conversation among Western monks to refer to desires, as in 'sugar kilesa,' 'sleep kilesa,' 'robe kilesa,' etc.

Pong more complete in that Bhikkhu ordinations could be done there.

One of the Westerners who showed up at this time was Gary, a layman from California. I think Luang Por took a special interest in him, which in practical terms meant that he made life difficult for him, thereby leaving a few good stories for posterity.

Gary was a clinical psychologist, in his late 30's. He'd studied Zen a little, had been in Japan recently, didn't seem particularly sure about what he was going to do next. After a short stay he had to leave as his visa was about to expire. We were outside the sala after evening chanting when he told me that he was leaving the next day. I was just about to head back to my kuti when I had a sudden intuition and asked, why don't you go and take leave of Ajahn Chah? So I went to Luang Por's kuti with him. I told Luang Por that Gary was leaving and had come to pay respects. Luang Por immediately zeroed in on him. He asked what his occupation was. Psychologist is "mind-scientist" in Thai. "The mind-scientist dies because of the mind," Ajahn Chah said. Pause. "The boxer dies because of boxing ... The snake doctor dies because of the snake. ... The mind scientist dies because of the mind. ... Understand?"

I translated this, and then he went on. "You can see this mind at work. Is it you? Is it yours?" "I don't know if it's me or mine, but it's certainly out of control" was Gary's answer.

That's it, said Luang Por. The mind is like a monkey, he continued, always jumping around, never content. "It goes upstairs, and it gets bored, so then it runs downstairs, but it gets bored there too. It has bad food and it gets tired of that, then you give it good food but it tires of that. So it goes to a movie, but ... " In Buddhist practice, he explained, we stop nurturing the monkey. Rather we nurture mental stability. We stop feeding the monkey, let it wear itself out and die. "This is called 'a dead monkey.' The dead monkey rots away, then it's called 'a monkey's bones.'"

Luang Por was right on target, it was one of those occasions when you felt that the whole kuti was filled with light, and I could see that Gary appreciated what was being said to him. We took our leave, and when I said good night to him, he said, "I think I'll come back here after I get my visa renewed." Of course I'd heard that before, but he actually did come back and ended up ordaining and staying for almost three years.

One of the well-known Gary stories concerns Luang Por's advice to the brokenhearted. Gary had a girlfriend back home, and thought that he might want to go back and marry her someday—he had entered monastic life without a sense of long-term commitment. Then the "Dear John" letter came; she had married someone else. I wasn't there at the time, but others said Gary was pretty upset. One day someone mentioned it to Luang Por. With his merciless compassion, he advised Gary to write to the woman and ask her to send her a vial with some of her shit in it. Then whenever he thought of her with longing, he should open the vial and smell it.

The visa business taken care of, I wanted to leave Wat Bah Pong for a more secluded place, but wasn't sure where to go. In those days Luang Por said that he wouldn't allow more than one farang to live in any of the branches. Ajahn Jun's wat, Beung Kow Luang, was where I wanted to go, but there was a farang monk there already. One night I went to Luang Por's kuti. He was talking with a few monks. Wat Bah Klor needed a monk. He looked at me and asked if I wanted to go. I had liked the place when I was there but hadn't thought about returning there to stay. I said I'd like to go, but was thinking about going somewhere to make a new umbrella for my mosquito net. He pulled one out from under his seat and said, you can have this one. When do I go, I asked. Tomorrow after the meal. So that was that.

I went in a car with an old Laotian monk whom Luang Por called Por Siang Noy ("Father Little Sound", i.e. high-pitched voice). He was small, a ball of energy, and pretty funny (though I'm not sure he intended to be). We were met at the wat by another old monk, Por Boon, a *Dhammayut* monk from Nakorn Panom, seemingly the exact opposite of Por Siang Noy: tall and thin, quiet, dignified. All his actions seemed so meticulous and mindful, not a drop of energy wasted. I began to think after a while, if there's an arhat in Thailand, it's Por Boon. Por Siang Noy was visible and audible, his output of energy obvious. I sat between them. They complemented each other perfectly, it seemed. We got along well. Only a few lay people came, the food was adequate. We didn't do much work or group practice. Somehow I felt more content as a bhikkhu than I had ever felt, one morning even feeling joyous (!). It was a combination of factors, but the company of the two old gents was something special. Ajahn Chah had said that as a young monk he liked to live with the old *"Luang Tah,"* (elderly monks) asking them what it was like to be old and nearer to death. Now I found myself enjoying the peacefulness of the two men who had nowhere else to go, and marvelling at their energy—they went on the longer pindapat while I took the shorter route; when the leaves started to fall they would go out early in the afternoon and sweep for hours. Hot season was trying to begin, and I began to drag my tail. The old guys were running rings around me. One evening before chanting, Por Siang Noy and I were drinking tea with sugar. Por Boon abstained, as he usually did. "If I drink it, it just makes me hot," he said. I said that it made me hot, too, but at least it gave me some energy.

"An old person and a youngster are really different," he said. "An old man had aches and pains and felt tired yesterday, he feels the same today, and he knows he'll feel the same tomorrow. He sees home, he knows the end of the road is near, so things don't matter. But to a young man they still matter." This was very revealing to me, it helped me to understand how so many of the old monks I'd lived with were able to practice so hard.

Por Boon was the senior monk but didn't feel inclined to give desanas to the handful of people who came on Wun Pra, but Por Siang Noy would occasionally talk without waiting for a request. Once he gave a brief talk on meditation. "The mind is fast; the defilements are just a little slower ... You want to know what defilement is? I'll explain it for you. A man once went to an Ajahn to learn how to meditate. The Ajahn said, 'sit still and repeat "Buddho" to yourself.' After a while, the Ajahn asked, 'OK, while you were sitting there trying to concentrate on "Buddho" what did your mind think about?' The man answered, 'I kept on thinking about a flashlight bulb.' That's it, that's defilement: a flashlight bulb."

In late February (1975) we all returned to Wat Bah Pong for Magha Puja and the funeral of Ajahn Chah's mother. Luang Por had allowed a huge number of temporary novice ordinations for the occasion. Some of those who ordained were longtime lay supporters, and a few of them stayed in robes for the long term. There were

85

two successive nights of desanas. The second night I was doing walking meditation outside the sala when Luang Por came out the back door. It was late, the crowd had thinned out, and he was alone, so I went up to him to escort him back to his kuti. As he walked away from the sala, he said "'Anicca-dukkha-anatta'*—I can't listen to any more." It was encouraging to know that the Chief himself didn't take these ordeals too seriously.

As soon as the ceremonies were done with, I asked permission to go to Beung Kow Luang. I arrived there at the beginning of a very hot and dry hot season. And I was just in time for another funeral. A young monk, Boonrawt, had gotten malaria, which went to his brain and killed him. The body was being kept in the sala. One of Ajahn Jun's favorite slogans had always been, it's better to die than disrobe; better to disrobe than slack off the practice. So now he was saying, "You see? Boonrawt made it, he died in the yellow robes." Something to aspire to, that was.

After I'd been there a few days, Ajahn Tieng showed up one evening. He was the senior-most disciple of Ajahn Chah, abbot of the first branch monastery of Wat Bah Pong, and Ajahn Jun's crony. I was happy to see him, since he came with an entourage of lay people, who had brought a big bucket of iced coffee. I paid my respects, downed a few mugs, and took my seat for evening chanting. After we chanted, Ajahn Tieng told the nuns to do some chanting, Dhammacakkappavattana Sutta with translation and a few other favorites. Then he took the microphone that had been set up, leaned back on his fat cushion, and started talking. An inspired funeral desana. Listening to desanas wasn't my favorite pastime, but when they were talking about death I always felt I had to put my likes and dislikes aside, it was something I had to listen to. After two hours he stopped, so I went back to my kuti for some yoga, but I soon heard his voice over the loudspeaker again. I guess he had just stopped to catch his breath. After another two hours, he handed the microphone to Ajahn Jun, who spoke for three hours. Then it was dawn, so we went on pindapat. Just another working day in the life of a bhikkhu. At midday, just as I was getting comfortable, someone

---

* Impermanence, suffering and not self, the Three Characteristics of existence, and the subject most commonly used for talks at funerals.

came to drag me out of my kuti so I could stand out in the hot sun and chant while they set fire to the body. Then afternoon chores, a bath, a brief rest, and a meeting in the bote. Ajahn Tieng was still there. "Varapanyo! Stay up all night?" he asked me. Yes, I did, I answered. "No," he said, "I mean tonight." Well, I hadn't really thought about it, I meekly said in desperation.

He was off and running. "If you don't sleep tonight, you can sleep tomorrow night. If you don't sleep tomorrow night, you can sleep the night after ... " He sent for the nuns, they did the chanting routine, he began another desana. Around 2 AM I gave up and went to get some sleep.

Although Ajahn Jun wasn't doing much teaching or training, there was good energy in the daily routine of the wat. The bell rang at 3 AM, as elsewhere, but everyone was sitting in the sala by 3:10. I would have to move as fast as I could, with no time for thinking or for the famous Beung Kow Luang mosquitoes to get me. I would half-run to the sala in order not to be the last one there, or at least not to get there too long after all the others. Everything, including eating, was done briskly. Without much talk, everyone did their share to keep the practice going. Occasionally Ajahn Jun would give us a desana, usually in the scolding *Isan* manner. Once he said, you guys should have lived with Luang Por. I'm easygoing, but he was really ferocious. That was very interesting; most monks seemed to be terrified of Ajahn Jun, whereas most of the farang experienced Luang Por as the kindly grandfather.

One evening on Wun Pra, as we began to sit after chanting, Ajahn Jun said, get in a good meditation posture and make up your minds to sit there until dawn, without getting up. Then as we sat, he began to scold us about almost everything. Eating, sleeping, daily routine. Naturally, I took it personally, except for when he talked about smoking. After two hours he rang the bell, so we could get up. "You fraud," I thought, though I was glad that we didn't have to continue sitting without moving. But I had taken his desana to heart, or so I thought, and felt guilty and upset for the rest of the all-nighter (perhaps a classic example of grabbing the snake by the tail). Since he had talked so much about greedy eating, I determined that I wouldn't stuff myself as I liked to do after the all night practice. I hardly ate anything, was the first one finished (no mean feat in that wat), and as soon as I saw Ajahn Jun finish eating, I jumped off my seat to take his bowl for cleaning. "What's the matter?" he said, "You ate so little." That made me feel a little foolish, it made me reconsider what the previous night had been all about. Later on, when I was with Ajahn Sumedho at Wat Bung Wai and hearing the teaching in my own language and idiom, I began to get a new perspective on all of this, and this one episode stood out in my memory.

After I'd been there a few weeks, two high school friends came to visit me, they also arriving in time for a funeral, this one for a village woman. I had known one of them since age three. His personality and the life he'd been leading were a vivid contrast to what I'd been doing as a monk. It made things very clear for me. In a monastery you often feel like you're just plodding along, putting in time. You may get obsessed with little problems or with your own shortcomings, and sink down into the feeling that not much is happening, and perhaps it's just plain hopeless. Then you get a look at how people live on the outside, how confused they are, seeking happiness but because of their ignorance finding only suffering. You look back at yourself again, realize you're following a true path, see how much you've accomplished already. This was such an instance. In addition to that, I could see that my friend needed help, so I suggested he stay for a while. This really terrified him. He had had some idealistic picture in his mind of what I was doing there, and thought he could come and get some instant transmission that would open the pearly gates for him. When he saw how we actually lived, it wasn't so romantic. I suggested he stay for the two months of his visa, then one month, then two weeks, one week, a few days … Ajahn Jun was very sympathetic and offered to make life as comfortable as possible for him, but Joe saw it as a death sentence, and after two days he left.

I felt like I was holding my own, keeping up with the pace of things in the wat, and it felt like something of an accomplishment in itself. Ajahn Tieng dropped in one afternoon, and when I went to pay respects, he asked if I was 'sabai' living there. I thought about it and answered that I was, and he said, that's good enough, you can settle for that. It seemed like a reasonable attitude. When times are hard one hopes for dramatic breakthroughs, but in fact the burdens gradually lighten, and peace and contentment build up without one's thinking about it too much or taking much notice.

Ajahn Tieng also mentioned that Ajahn Sumedho and a few farang monks had gone to live in some place near the railroad tracks, not far from Wat Bah Pong, and that they were establishing a monastery there.

In the beginning of May I got sick, a fever that wouldn't go away. I tried to hang in there but occasionally would come late to morning practice. One morning Ajahn Jun was there. He led the chanting, and we did the *Paritta* ("protection") chants, including the *Bojjhango* (for curing illness). He would often talk between chants, and this time he said, "The novice has a stomach problem, may he get better. The monk has a fever but he sleeps late, may he not get better." Very comforting.

Some relatives of mine were planning to visit me at Wat Bah Pong later in the month, so I went there to meet them. When I first went to see Luang Por and he asked me how I was, I mentioned that I'd been sick for a while, but he didn't seem too concerned. A few days later I finally went in to town to see a doctor, and much to my surprise found out it was malaria. I had gone to the army hospital, where the head doctor was a longtime supporter of Luang Por, and after the blood test he checked the results himself, so I could be pretty sure the diagnosis was correct (he said that the guy at the microscope was an alcoholic and his hands shook, so you never knew if his readings were right).

I was surprised by this and a little worried too. I remembered Ajahn Sumedho saying how he'd always thought of malaria as something dreadful, "written in big red letters." I'd seen several monks with malaria, some of them extremely ill, and I knew of two who'd died of it. So when I got back to the Wat and checked in at Luang Por's kuti, I didn't wait to be acknowledged—he was speaking to some lay people—but I just blurted out, "Luang Por, they say I've got malaria." From a few hundred miles away, he coolly said, "they say what they say," or something like that.

I began taking the medicine "they" had given me, but it didn't seem to do much good, and after two or three days the condition started getting worse. It became difficult to eat or sleep, leaving me with little to do but lie around my kuti in restless lethargy. I think that what I dreaded most about getting ill in the wat was not the illness itself, but the long days of lying in the kuti with nothing to do, nothing to distract the attention and no energy to do formal meditation. Now it was happening.

Early one afternoon, unable to peacefully convalesce, I walked out to the eating hall where a Canadian monk was sewing robes for some farang novices who were about to ordain as bhikkhus, and where others would gather as well. Soon someone was calling me from the front of the sala—my relatives had arrived. In a somewhat spaced-out state, I went to meet them. My uncle stuck out his hand, but instead of shaking it, I just looked at it hanging out there—it was a long time since I'd shaken hands with anyone or even seen anyone shake hands, and he caught me by surprise. Then as a greeting, I said, "Where'd you get all that hair?" He'd been bald as long as I'd known him, and now he was sporting a toupee.

Formalities completed, I decided to take them over to Wat Bung Wai to meet Ajahn Sumedho and let him do the talking; also, I hadn't been there yet and wanted to see it. They were fairly curious and had some good questions to ask. It was inspiring to watch Ajahn Sumedho talking with them, with his gift for explaining things to people in language they could understand, without watering down the message. This period was also when he first began talking about some day going to the West, something he'd never been interested in before. I felt a confident, positive atmosphere at Bung Wai and decided to go there for the vassa.

But in the meanwhile I had to entertain my relatives for another two days and deal with the malaria. One night, lying in my kuti, unable to sleep, I got a little touch of delirium. I'd just read *Journey to Ixtlan,* and the forest seemed to be electric with mysterious energies and menacing forces. Then I thought, this is pretty strange: I took the medicine they prescribed me, and I'm getting worse. ... Malaria is serious business. ... That other monk at Beung Kow Luang died from it, and he was stronger than I am ... maybe I could die from it ... maybe I could die tonight.

By now I was beside myself with fear. Finally I managed to catch myself. I realized it was my own creation, so trying to keep mindful, lying in the "Lion's Posture," I began bringing up the thoughts and watching the chain reaction, over and over until I could see it clearly and step back from it. I got to a point of equanimity where the terror of thinking about death was gone, and thought that if my time had really come, perhaps I was ready. Then the thought, well, I could die now, but my parents would be upset; and I got a look at various forces that pull one back to the world, to life, to birth in various states.

That night was a lot of fun, but the next day I was back to the physical reality of "dragging a corpse around." Like all things, my equanimity passed away. I went to the public malaria clinic in Ubon and got some new medicine. Then I plucked up a mixture of self-pity and courage and went to see Luang Por. I asked him to forgive me for bothering him, but I was in pretty bad shape, and I wondered if I should get some kind of sedative to enable me to sleep. He immediately put up his hand and said, you take those things, you'll ruin your brain. When it's time to sleep, you'll sleep, he assured me.

Then he said, "I saw that you were sick. Don't worry, you're not going to die. ... Were you afraid you'd die?" I answered that I'd thought about it; I'd never had malaria before, the symptoms were a little frightening, etc.

He laughed at this, and then said, "It's an opportunity to meditate anew."

I'm going into detail on this episode for the reason that living in the tropics exposes one to various diseases, and like anything else, illness became part of the practice when it occurred. Most of the Western monks who stayed for a while experienced one or more serious illnesses, and I think most would consider it a valuable experience. Coming as we did from our comfortable, germfree backgrounds, these diseases could be quite terrifying to our habitual way of thinking. Dependable medical care was not readily available in that neck of the woods, and Ajahn Chah was constantly pointing out to us how obsessed we were with our bodies. Endurance was an important part of his training. He once said to some Thai monks at his kuti, "You guys don't feel well, so you go to see the doctors, and they tell you you're malnourished. It's true; so what can you do about it?"

After reassuring me that I wasn't going to die, he said "I had malaria for three years." I'd heard the stories before, about how in

91

the early days of Wat Bah Pong everybody got malaria, and there was simply no way to get treatment for it. But now it really hit home. Contemplating even another three days was difficult for me, but three years … ?

Changing his tone and the subject, he very pleasantly asked me about my relatives and their visit. I related to him the story of my cousin, their daughter, who had been mugged and shot in New York City. As she was waiting for help, she used a meditation technique she had learned to slow down her bodily processes, and that was probably what saved her life. Luang Por showed interest in this, and as usual, he found the handle on it, picked it up, and gave me a beating with it. "You see? Your cousin was nearly dead but she could meditate. But Varapanyo has a *tiny* bit of fever and he's all upset and can't practice. … "

At least he did say that I could ask the kitchen to prepare rice gruel for me in the morning. The medicine finally started working, the fever abated. But I was pretty weak and had to take it easy for a while. I'd always had a reputation for taking it easy, I suppose, but now I couldn't even go through the motions and pretend that I was maintaining the normal routine. Over the years I'd come to depend on that routine, it imposed some kind of order and kept my mind from getting too chaotic; but now I had to step back and find something else to do with my time. As I mentioned, the thought of this had always been a frightening unknown, but at this point I found myself able to relax mentally in a way I'd never done before. It was one of those times when I could look back and see the changes that had occurred, and also, for the first time, I felt I had an overview of the "five year plan." I could see that it was a realistic period of time to allot for training the mind and overhauling one's views and habits (at this point I had been in robes about four and a half years, and was about to enter my fourth vassa as a bhikkhu). Luang Por had often spoken of Right View and *Sila,* moral discipline, as the foundations of practice, and I could see how my habitual patterns of understanding and acting had been changed, and that I had some real appreciation of Sila, something that I and probably most Westerners didn't inherit as part of our upbringing.

So there was light at the end of the tunnel. I also started gaining back some of the weight and bodily strength that I'd lost shortly after ordaining. By the end of the vassa I was to become an object of wonderment, and jokes, because I'd become so fat. It felt like a heavy karmic burden that I'd been struggling with for years had been resolved.

As my strength came back I started hanging out with Luang Por more. Sometimes as we returned from pindapat, he would call my name just as I was ducking my head to walk past him and go on ahead, so I would just say *"Krup"* and fall into step behind him. One memorable morning he walked around the wall of the wat, from the back entrance to the front gate. Among other things, he asked me what it was like living with Ajahn Jun. I said I liked him and respected him as a teacher, but after a while I got tired of all the tough talk about *"toramahn"* (lit., "torture"). Luang Por asked, "Did Ajahn Jun 'toramahn' you very much?" No, he didn't, I answered, realizing it for the first time. "That's just his method of teaching," Luang Por said.

Then he asked me about Ajahn Sinuan. I said that when I first went to live with him, I had a very positive impression, but as time went on I began to agree with another monk who'd stayed with him, that he was somewhat lazy and liked to have a good time.

"Just like me," said Luang Por. "I really like to fool around … I've got a lot of defilements." Needless to say, this caught me off balance. Then he stopped walking, turned to look at me, and with his inimitable timing and delivery said, "Listen, Varapanyo, I'm going to disrobe, and I want you to help me find a nice girl."

The man who was the comedian and the kindly grandfather could also be very tough. One afternoon I was at his kuti with an English monk, who expressed his weariness with the "toramahn" talk of the senior monks. Luang Por heard him out and then let him have it with both barrels. "When we were laymen we followed our impulses in everything. Did it bring happiness? What kind of practice can we have without patience and endurance? Sometimes I get angry and I want to beat you but I have to restrain myself …" I'd never heard him talk quite like that before.

On another evening a couple of Thai novices came to him to complain about the abbot of the branch monastery they'd been sent to—actually quite a bold thing for Thais to do (a sign of a changing society?). Their abbot was temperamental and imperious, he got angry if the bell wasn't rung on time, they had to ask permission of him to do little things. They made it sound pretty bad, and sitting there in the dark, I thought I sensed Luang Por listening in sympathy, concerned that one of his monasteries was being mismanaged. Then he came down on them, repeating their complaints in a mocking voice. Of course the bell should be rung on time; what's wrong with trying to make people do their duties properly? The abbot of a monastery is responsible for everything that goes on. According to the Vinaya, monks should ask permission to go pindapat, to study the Patimokkha, etc. Luang Por wasn't buying, he stood behind his abbots. He told the novices to go back there and not bother him with any more complaints.

V

"So the Guru is like the embodiment of the Buddha and is absolutely essential, and is the superior source of refuge in all times and in all situations."

Two days before vassa i went over to Wat Bung Wai. Wat Bung Wai is in itself a major chapter in Ajahn Chah's biography, and there are others who can tell its story in better detail. By this time the monks had been there about four months. The idea of having a farang wat had been in circulation for a while, but when it happened, it came about without planning, which is the way it usually happened with the growth of the branch monasteries. The merit and purity of the practice seemed to create appropriate situations.

Like Luang Por, Ajahn Sumedho could be tough or gentle. When I had returned from Beung Kow Luang, he was visiting Wat Bah Pong. I was talking with another monk about my uncertainty as to where to spend vassa, and we got into rehashing our doubts. Suddenly Ajahn Sumedho interrupted. In a most forceful tone, he said "None of you are willing to give up a fucking thing. Not one of you. Life is dull in these monasteries, it's boring. Luang Por says you have to die."

But usually his talk was clear and simple, almost comforting. He was pointing at the essence of the practice, which is seeing the Three Characteristics. He said he felt that there was generally too much emphasis on the tough talk and the ascetic side of the practice, without getting at the heart of the matter. Luang Por himself, he said, had begun to say that the *toramahn* methods of the "old days" of Wat Bah Pong had not really produced satisfactory results. Especially for Westerners, who tended to be guilt-ridden and compulsive about meditation, this didn't seem to be the best approach. Informal talks that he gave when he visited Wat Bah Pong before vassa had been very refreshing to me. Something clicked inside me, and I realized that I was doing what I was supposed to be doing, i.e. observing the three characteristics, and that I need not be anxious about the undefinable something else that I usually felt I was failing to do.

On the first night of vassa, Ajahn Sumedho told us what the schedule would be—the emphasis would clearly be on formal meditation practice, not on the endless Vinaya readings, talks, and work projects that went on in most of the branch monasteries—and encouraged us to just do the practice as it was set up, without second thoughts, and that if we did so, mindfulness would become habitual, and we'd find that we'd be able to live our lives out mindfully. That sounded reasonable to me, and quite wonderful—what more could a person ask for, really? But it still seemed a distant goal.

There was also more of a harmony of purpose than I'd felt before—no temporary ordinations, kids who were in the monastery only because their parents had sent them—and easy communication with each other, without cultural barriers that often could lead to misunderstanding and bad feeling. This is not to say that everything was perfect, of course. We had much to learn about living with each other, and Ajahn Sumedho had many trials and lessons about being a teacher waiting for him. Still, the overall feeling was very good, and there were many factors that hadn't been present in past situations in other places.

The vassa went on, the schedule intensified. It wasn't easy, but it was good. Meanwhile, our fame was spreading. When lay people went to see Luang Por, he would ask them if they'd seen Sumedho's wat yet. Added to the already solid support of the Bung Wai villagers, all these townspeople coming with food (and often seeking lottery numbers) made for a pretty substantial diet, and most of us started getting fat, especially me. Luang Por would make

Ajahn Chah, Ajahn Sumedho, and the Western monks, novices and laymen at Wat Bah Bung Wai (Wat Nanachat), 1975.

his usual jokes, calling it "Wat Bah Woon Wai" ("Forest Monastery of Confusion") or "Wat Bah Amerikawat," but he obviously thought it was a good thing, and the lay people who came did, too. Yet I doubt anyone could have envisioned how the place would develop in the near future. That first vassa there were only nine or ten kutis and two "gadorp" (grass huts with no floor, just a bed on the ground). Ajahn Sumedho lived in a small bamboo kuti with a grass roof, and we had a tiny grass-roofed sala with a dirt floor.

Luang Por came for a visit one afternoon during the vassa. Lay people came at night, and there were the usual Dharma talks. After they had gone home, we were sitting with Luang Por, and he directed us to set up a bed in the open for him. "I'll sleep here," he said, "and Varapanyo will massage my feet all night." It was absurd, of course, but I had to do it. He lay down and I went to work. He seemed to doze off but would then start talking to me. After a few hours one of the monks offered to replace me for a bit so I could go do yoga. Luang Por was sound asleep at that point, but the monk told me that as soon as I had gone, he woke up and said "Where's Varapanyo? He didn't go to sleep, did he?"

I returned to finish my vigil. Luang Por was going to eat in a house, but he gave us a talk at dawn. He had a manner of knowing that the world waits for him, and it didn't matter that faithful villagers were waiting to put food in the bowls of hungry monks. One monk who was a relative newcomer had realized that he had committed a *Sanghadisesa* offense a long time ago, so he told Ajahn Sumedho, who told Luang Por. Luang Por took it a lot better than he usually did—it was one of the few things that seemed to put him in a wrathful way. He reminded us of the scriptural analogy of putting "it" in the mouth of a cobra, and told us to contemplate that in times of lust. In the months to come there would be a few other monks who found themselves with a similar problem, and there were a few pithy and hilarious comments from Luang Por, but perhaps it is neither necessary nor appropriate to go into the details here. Suffice it to say that in time the Sangha at Bung Wai learned to do the *Parivasa* process, as we learned to do other Sangha functions.

This was the first time I had spent a vassa without thinking about where I would go afterwards. Wat Bung Wai was just the place where I was living, rather than a place of exile. Though I didn't quite feel I had "attained" to being able to live out my life mindfully, perhaps there really was something to what Ajahn Sumedho had said at the vassa's beginning. (On the night after vassa ended, Ajahn Sumedho asked us each to say something about how we felt about the previous months' experience. A young monk who was soon to lose his marbles and disrobe was the one to say he was now able to live out his life thus. His dignified bearing and seemingly impeccable mindfulness had been noticed by all, even Luang Por; I used to say to myself, "Why can't you be more like him?" It was a classic example of the pitfalls of watching others, attaching to concepts, etc.).

That year Luang Por didn't make the rounds of the kathina ceremonies at the branch monasteries, as he usually did. It was another sign of his aging. In 1971 and '72 he was a young man. He would sweep leaves with us for hours, and often go on the longest pindapat, and he was constantly travelling to the branch monasteries, which were just starting to proliferate then. By 1975 he seemed to have aged about 10 years. A year later, when work on the bote was in full swing, he would come out to oversee, but couldn't do much physically. One monk remarked how painful it was to watch him as he bent down to pick up a scrap of wood; he was clearly losing the battle against old age.

He did come to our Pah Bah ceremony, however. It was a pretty humble affair, sponsored by the local railroad workers. They gave us each a blanket and a lantern. I remember how I prized those new acquisitions then. But life was never again to be so austere there. Ajahn Sumedho had observed, with regret, that we would probably never have the experience of lacking for anything. (I didn't regret the prospect so much, but I was never as keen on asceticism as Ajahn Sumedho was).

Ajahn Sumedho gave the first desana of the Pah Bah. He talked about how some monks liked chanting and some didn't, some preferred to do a lot of sitting meditation while others liked to walk more, some agonized over whether or not it was permissible to eat cheese after noon. On and on and on. Most of us became bored and restless as he talked; there didn't seem to be much point to it. After he was finished, Luang Por spoke from his seat in a heavy, serious tone to the lay people. "I don't think you understand what Tahn Sumedho was talking about. Probably not even one of you." And he went on to talk about non-discrimination, the question of the person who isn't going forward, isn't moving backwards, isn't standing still. Where is he? The next day Ajahn Sumedho said that his desana had been meant for Luang Por; he wanted to show him that somebody understood what he taught. He thought that would be the best gift he could give him. As Ajahn Sumedho came into his own as a teacher, one clearly had the impression of him as the man in charge, so it was always very moving to get these reminders of his devotion to his own master.

VI

"You should understand that all spiritual attainments come from the Guru. It is a result of his transmission and his blessing which you receive as his disciple."

After the kathina season was over, Luang Por sent Ajahn Sumedho and another monk to Ayuthaya to study about *parivasa*. This left me minding the shop for two weeks. I was only a four vassa monk, and certainly not a teacher, but all went smoothly. Such occasions always increased my reverence for the brilliance of the Vinaya and the way it was used in Ajahn Chah's wat; just applying ourselves to the daily routine and the monastic discipline was enough to keep everything functioning harmoniously. This particular occasion showed me how much I and others had grown. Even giving the required *desanas* to the lay people (in Lao) became easy.

One afternoon Luang Por came to visit with a wealthy patroness. She seemed uncertain as to who this senior farang monk was, so Luang Por introduced me. "Ajahn Varapanyo," he intoned. "He's seen the Dharma, realized the Dharma." I felt like crawling under the seat. He spoke in such a serious way. But of course we all knew how much such praise was worth. Over the years I found that he would praise me a few times and I would start to look forward to seeing him, then the next time he would throw shit all over me, often in front of a group of people, which could be quite humiliating and infuriating.

The flow of new farang monks, visiting laymen, and families of monks was increasing at that time. There was a similar feeling whenever a monk's parents visited. They obviously appreciated what was going on there, yet one could see that they'd much rather have their sons escape from this fate worse than death. Another similarity was something Ajahn Sumedho had long talked about, that most of us came from stable families with some basic moral values—in other words, we were "sons of good families," as the scriptures would say. After disrobing and getting a look at all the broken marriages and children who were shuttled back and forth from one parent to the other, and American youth who seemed to be evolving into a generation of ghouls, this took on added meaning for me.

Before the vassa I had received a letter from my grandmother expressing her wish that I would be in New York for my grandparents' 60th anniversary the following year. My first thought was "Good luck, Granny"—I hadn't left Ubon in two and a half years, and could hardly conceive of going to Bangkok, much less the U.S. But then I considered it: maybe I could have them invite Luang Por as well, since before completing five vassa I really shouldn't travel by myself anyhow, and it might be the beginning of spreading his teaching to the West. When I mentioned it to him, it still seemed unreal to me, and all he said was that I couldn't go home when I was so skinny, it would give people a bad idea about Buddhism.

But some time after the vassa I mentioned it to Ajahn Sumedho, and one day he asked me if he could go in Luang Por's place, if the trip were really possible and Luang Por didn't want to go. Ajahn Sumedho hadn't seen his elderly parents for 12 years, and he had a standing invitation from a sponsor to pay his fare. Perhaps he also sensed that the time might be right for going to the West. We discussed it at Christmas time with Luang Por, who said he wasn't sure if he could go; then at Magha Puja we asked him for a decision, since we had to start making plans. He said he was too busy with the bote; maybe next year. So Ajahn Sumedho would go with me.

In the meantime I suddenly became very sick with fever, aching, and nausea. I didn't eat for a few days, and when I didn't appear for evening coffee the others knew that I must really be ill. But such was the state of things that I didn't even consider going to a doctor or the Ubon hospital—not trying to be heroic, but because local medical care was, at its best, only slightly better than nothing, and the trip to town itself was quite an ordeal (the road that ran by the monastery was just in the process of being paved then). During the vassa a few monks had gotten sick, gone to the hospital, were tested for everything the docs could think of, and after several days, when the symptoms had subsided, somebody would decide that it was probably typhoid fever ... which was what the villagers thought I had now, so they brought me gallon jugs of herbal medicine which tasted like detergent. It didn't do any harm, and the fever went down after a few days, but the nausea remained.

Then we got word that some Air Force people would be coming to "*tam boon*" (make merit, i.e. offer food). They arrived one morning before the meal and walked around the wat. When they gathered in the sala, they seemed to be quite blown away, having seen the simplicity in which we lived. To middle class Bangkok people like them, Northeast Thailand was like Siberia, so how could we from the Western Paradises live like this? They immediately took up a collection to start building a proper sala, and another collection to help with the expenses of our planned trip to the U.S.

That evening Ajahn Sumedho and I took the train to Bangkok with some of them and a local supporter, Pansak (himself a retired Air Force officer) so that we could check out possible discounts for plane tickets. I had asked the "doctor" from the local health station for something to prevent motion sickness; he asked me what my symptoms were and listened thoughtfully as I described them. He returned that evening to take us to the station, gave me some Dramamine, and said, "Ajahn Varapanyo, what you have is called 'gas in the stomach'."

We were invited to stay at a place near the airport which some Air Force people had built for monks to use. Mercifully, our new patrons, Colonel Sak and Mae Bow, had our seats changed to a sleeper. In the morning we went to their house for the meal. Though the food was excellent, I could hardly touch it. Mae Bow noticed that I didn't look too well, and asked if I'd like to see a doctor. Then we set off with Pansak. First we went to the home of General Chu, the head of Thai International. His wife was there and gave us some information. In those days they didn't fly to the U.S. We went to Air Siam, a new airline. The director, Captain Tawee, was an ardent practicer and a follower of some of the Northeastern Ajahns, but he'd never seen farang monks before. He seemed quite moved, and said that he'd give us free tickets to California. We found out later that they were his own tickets; each year he and his wife could take a trip anywhere the airline flew to, and right there on the spot he decided to give them away.

When word got back to Thai Inter, they also gave us free tickets from London to Bangkok. Then we thought that we could afford to take Pansak along as a steward, the faithful, generous, luckless patron who'd been so helpful for so many years. Air Siam gave him a ticket at one-third price, which was promptly matched by Thai International.

I got to see a doctor that first night. A real doctor. In about 90 seconds he diagnosed me as having hepatitis. He gave me some medicines and told me to get lots of rest. When Ajahn Sumedho returned to Ubon, Mae Bow invited me to stay at the small *sala* by her house while I recuperated.

This was a much different situation from anything I'd experienced as a monk. I was on my own, in close proximity to lay people, surrounded by all the luxuries a bhikkhu could imagine. The residential area that I walked through every morning for pindapat resembled suburban America more than it did rural Thailand, or even the neighborhoods around the wats in Bangkok. But it all went quite smoothly. I felt like I knew how to use the Vinaya to keep a proper distance from it all and to maintain my practice, but without becoming uptight. I'm sure I couldn't have done that a couple of years before then. It was another positive sign, and gave me confidence for the trip to the U.S.

It was also refreshing for me to have a change of scene from the poverty-stricken Northeast. When I'd been at Wat Bah Klor, where the soil was more fertile and the villagers a little better off than at places like Nong Hy, I began to think that when living conditions were too harsh, it sometimes kept the mind in a rough state. Of course it's a matter of individual temperament and what a person may need at a particular point in time; sometimes Luang Por himself would talk about the four *sappaya,* the necessity of having suitable food, dwelling, climate, and people, whereas at other times he would urge practicers to seek out adverse conditions. At any rate, I rather enjoyed my convalescence in these celestial surroundings, and kept busy by translating "Entrance to the Vinaya", Volume III, for the Somdet of Wat Boworn.

Finally the time came to return to Ubon. It was mid-April, and we would be leaving for California in early May. I wasn't sick, but still weak, and the doctor had warned me to be careful about overexertion lest I damage my liver, which can take two months to two years to get back to normal after hepatitis. I got a ride in a car with Pansak and a friend of his, we arrived in the evening, and I decided to go out to Wat Bah Pong and pay my respects to Luang Por before going to Bung Wai. It was extremely hot, it had been a long day, and I was on wobbly legs. Work was going on at the bote site. We found Luang Por, who immediately started giving me the business. "So you've come back, you lazy guy ... Look how fat you are. I'll put you to work pounding earth, that's what you need ... " Just to look at one of those pounders was painful. My defenses were low, and I didn't find this very amusing. Sometimes he liked to make you feel miserable before you even got a chance to sit down, it seemed. The next morning I went on the short pindapat, and as we waited for him at the first houses, he walked up, pointed at me, and said to a new bhikkhu, "This one's already dead. Look how fat he is. Dead!" And the following morning, he started talking about how much trouble I was. "I could have twenty other monks, and they'd be less trouble than one of you." I seriously began to wonder if I'd worked my way into his doghouse somehow, though I couldn't think of any real misdeeds I'd committed recently; I hadn't even been at Wat Bah Pong for nine months. It was quite heavy, and the feeling remained with me even during the trip to the U.S., and it wasn't until my father told me that Ajahn Sumedho had said that I was one of Luang Por's favorites, and that therefore he liked to tease me, that I felt reassured.

Our trip had been intended for the purpose of visiting our families, but in Bangkok and then in the U.S. people asked Ajahn Sumedho to talk to them. He would often seem to be struggling as he began, but after a few minutes would get comfortable, get a feeling for what was appropriate to the occasion, and you could feel the room light up with interest. I was especially impressed by the way he was able to talk to lay people in the U.S., because he'd been away for so long.

Just before leaving California for New York, I tore the cartilage in my knee, so when Ajahn Sumedho returned to Thailand via England, I stayed in New York to have surgery. It turned out that Ajahn Sumedho had gone to stay at the Thai Wat in London, feeling that it would be the appropriate place to stay even though the English Sangha Trust house had been recommended to us; but the Thai Wat was very crowded, so he left after a day and went to the EST place, where it seems they had been waiting and hoping for a proper bhikkhu to show up. He made a big impression on them, and when I stopped there in August, they were preparing to go to Thailand and invite Ajahn Chah to send some monks to live there. So without planning, another situation had developed for spreading the Dharma.

I stayed in my parents' house for two months after Ajahn Sumedho left, and I again found I could keep the Vinaya without getting uptight over it. In general, the yellow robes and elaborate code of rules didn't seem to be as strange to people as I would have thought. In California I had seen and heard of several groups of people practicing in different Buddhist traditions. This was quite a change from when I'd left seven years before, and in Thailand I'd heard a little of the news but didn't have any accurate idea of the extent of it. In the suburbs of New York, however, such things were not to be found, and I looked forward to getting back to Thailand and the forest.

VII

"It is taught that even if you meditate for ten million kalpas, or undertake one million sadhanas, just one moment's remembrance of the Guru surpasses all this."

My knee was slow to heal, so I waited and returned to enter the second vassa,* a month after the rest of the Sangha had entered, still walking with a cane. Mike, a layman interested in ordaining, travelled with me from New York, and we took the train to Ubon together. Arriving at Wat Bah Pong, I was very moved to be back, and, full of reverence, went to see Luang Por. But as he saw me approaching his kuti, he started shouting at me. "No good, I won't have it. I don't want it—too fat! I won't have it … " In silence I kneeled clumsily on one knee, the closest I could come to prostrating. He quizzically asked, "Like that, huh?" and continued with his torrent of abuse. "What did you do, live in your mother's kitchen? You've got to fast … Fast for a week … Eat leaves for a month … "

An unsmiling, tight-lipped Ajahn Liem, who was second in charge now, showed me to my kuti. I was exhausted from the train and from Luang Por's verbal flogging, so I decided to skip the meal. Though fasting had always been uncomfortable for me, I fasted four

---

* The vassa, rains retreat, can be formally determined by a monk either on the full moon of the eighth lunar month, or the full moon of the ninth lunar month, the latter known as 'entering the second vassa.'

days, and started fasting a day or two every week. The sudden change of climate and the drastic change in diet left me with little appetite (and I did have plenty of weight to spare). Every morning when I looked into my bowl before the meal began, it was a grim sight to behold; I would think of the words of a once-popular song, "You don't know how lucky you are, boys/Back in the USSR." (After I disrobed and went to visit Mike, I heard him telling some friends of his about the food at Wat Bah Pong. "Normally you couldn't *pay* me to eat that stuff. Some of those fish concoctions ... there's better looking stuff down at the bait shop.")

I had never spent vassa at Wat Bah Pong, and this was the long awaited Number Five, but it was all rather anticlimactic. I felt reasonably comfortable as a bhikkhu by this time, so I didn't feel like I was struggling to cross a finish line anymore. Luang Por wasn't teaching much, and I couldn't take part in the group practice because of my knee—even at meal time I sat outside the eating hall where I could let my bad leg hang over the edge of the seat. Actually there wasn't even much group practice because of the work on the bote, mostly just building up the hill on which it was to sit. Some of the monks would work during the day, then everyone would come out following afternoon chores and continue long past dark, sometimes until midnight: One night I walked out to have a look, and Mike, who was carrying dirt and dripping sweat, looked up at me and said, "My Asian holiday." With Luang Por, of course, work was part of practice, like anything else. In his approach to practice you didn't just do what was "normal" or "sensible," but pushed beyond ordinary limits to break habits of body and mind. So that's how we worked (I say "we" because as my knee healed I started working; though perhaps it's easier to appreciate Luang Por's methods from the safe distance my disability gave me through much of the vassa).

There were a few farang spending vassa at Wat Bah Pong, and they weren't getting any instruction, so I offered to teach Vinaya, which Luang Por approved. I had heard Vinaya teachings many times over and had read most of the Vinaya Pitaka, and had learned over the years how to use it properly, so I was confident I could teach it and also give some pointers on life in Luang Por's wat. I could see how the "system" itself prepares people for transmitting something to those who come later; and in the years since then, there have always been capable people to take charge at Wat Bung Wai and other places. Luang Por often used to ask his monks, if you can't practice properly and maintain harmony now, what will you do after I'm gone? Well, now he's gone even though his body lingers on, and I think most people are pleased with the way the Sangha has held together.

There wasn't a lot of time for hanging out with him due to the work on the bote, but I went pindapat with him and one old monk in the nun's village while my knee was still healing, and there were of course the occasional unforgettable vignettes. Once as I walked by his kuti after the chores (my kuti was in the forest behind his), he called out to me as he sat speaking with a monk. I knelt down on the ground, and he asked, "When you were in America, did women try to touch you?" No, that hadn't been a problem, I said. "Did people ask you why you couldn't touch women?" Yes, they did. "How did you answer them?" I explained that it was to help preserve the Brahmacariya, the celibate life. "Wrong answer," he said, and then after his theatrical pause: "You should have told them, 'if a monk touches a woman, he'll get a stomach ache'."

So the mythical five vassa had gone by, and it now seemed like it hadn't really been such a long time. When I first met Ajahn Sumedho, when I was a newly ordained novice, he said, "Life is short, so I want to do something good with my life." I said to him, "You really think life is short? To me it seems interminably long." But a couple of years later I started to notice the time going by quickly; it seemed like every time I turned around, another two weeks had passed and it was time to shave my head again. At Wat Nong Hy I started thinking, "only 29 months and three weeks until I enter my fifth vassa." And now it had come to pass. In many ways I felt like the same person, but big changes had occurred. It really seemed that my sojourning in the lower realms was behind me. Luang Por had often said that being "beyond dependence" didn't just mean hanging out for five years and then grabbing your bowl and taking off. Yet I often felt that I had done little more than hang out, or hang in, and I thought that just being in the wat and keeping the Vinaya would have a substantial effect on almost anyone.

George Sharpe of the English Sangha Trust arrived in December (1976). Luang Por was away, and though he had come to offer a *vihara* (monastic dwelling) and lay support, he received the usual "hospitality" from Ajahn Liem: sleeping in the sala, eating out of a grungy basin while sitting on the concrete outside the eating hall. I didn't even think about it, but Ajahn Sumedho was quite upset when he heard, especially since he later took a trip with George to see Ajahn Mahabua, where the treatment was much better (and Ajahn Mahabua has a reputation for giving guests a hard time). When I mentioned it to Luang Por, however, all he said was "we are not Mahabua."

Everyone knows how it turned out; Ajahn Mahabua didn't feel that any of his monks were ready to go to England, though he did emphasize that if he did send monks, the separation of Dhammayut and Mahanikaya sects would have to be maintained. Luang Por agreed to go in May with Ajahn Sumedho. An English monk, Khemadhammo, with whom I had ordained, was going to visit his parents, so he went along. Two other junior monks went to the U.S. and Canada and stopped in London afterwards; and Luang Por decided to leave them all there.

George would come to my kuti in the evening to drink cocoa and talk. He was going through some emotional upheaval at the time, in addition to the rigors of the trip and the battle he'd been fighting to salvage the English Sangha Trust. After talking for a long time on one of his first evenings there, he said "Well, I feel a bit better now, I was feeling rather disoriented and depressed for a while here." I said "I know what you mean. I felt that way the first two or three years I was here."

That was also the year of Luang Por's "Christ-Buddhamas" desana. The Sangha at Bung Wai had decided to celebrate Christmas and invited the lay people to join, and invited Luang Por also. As Jack Kornfield tells it, the lay people were a little skeptical or upset; why, they asked, were Buddhist monks celebrating Christmas? Luang Por, therefore, gave a talk on the purpose of religion. As far as he understood it, he said, Christianity taught people to do good and avoid evil, just as Buddhism did. So what was the problem? However, if people were upset by the idea of celebrating Christmas, that was easily remedied: we would no longer call it

Christmas. Let's call it "Christ-Buddhamas." As far as I know, having been there for a visit on December 25, 1981, the occasion is still celebrated with food offerings and desanas (and whether or not the story is perfectly true may not be so important—Luang Por himself used to embellish stories of other people's words and deeds, and adjust them to fit his purposes for teaching).

Ajahn Chah wasn't a student of comparative religion, he didn't know the teachings of other religions or other sects of Buddhism in detail, but he certainly had realization of what religion is all about, and he liked to emphasize that which was common to different religions, and to separate name from fact. When someone asked him why there was so much crime in Thailand, a Buddhist country, or why Indochina was such a mess, he said those aren't Buddhists doing those things, that isn't Buddhism doing those things; those are *people* doing those things. Buddha never taught anything like that.

He once mentioned that when he was a child, there were some Christian children in his school. When the kids would be playing in the school yard, one would shout, "I'm Buddhist," another would shout "I'm Christian," and a fight would break out. So this was what quarreling between religions amounted to: kids in the school yard fighting over names.

When 1977 began, I decided that I would like to go to Bangkok to get acupuncture for my knees, and then go tudong. Just at that time, an Australian monk showed up at Wat Bah Pong to take leave of Luang Por before going tudong. The night before he left I went to Luang Por's kuti, but sat behind the wall instead of joining the others sitting in front of Luang Por. He was talking to the monk about the benefits of tudong. I don't remember many of the details, mainly that he praised it, and said that even if one wasn't ready to "proclaim" the Dharma, one could proclaim the *Brahmacariya* ("Holy Life") through one's behavior, thereby inspiring faith in others, and he told a story about Sariputta, who was led to the Dharma by seeing a bhikkhu walking pindapat and feeling inspired by his dignified deportment.

The next night I went to see him, and told him of my plans. "Tudong? Why do you want to go tudong?" he said, and proceeded to expound on the uselessness of wandering around. It was a good example of how he didn't have stock answers for people. Maybe he wanted to test me. Maybe he really thought I shouldn't go. I think that good teachers hope that their disciples will eventually learn how to think for themselves (or how to *not* think, perhaps, and make their own decisions with a clear mind). He surprised me time and time again, and over the years I finally came to realize that he wasn't predictable. There was once a fellow named Ron, an arrogant young American, who came to Wat Bah Pong. He had gotten a grant to do a study of Buddhism, and as part of the project he was going to ordain for a while. He had come to interview Ajahn Chah. When I first took him to see Luang Por, I mentioned that he was planning to ordain, thinking that this would be pleasing to Luang Por, who usually would suggest to any farang visiting Wat Bah Pong that the only decent use of their time on earth would be to ordain. But to Ron he said "Why do you want to ordain? It's a lot of trouble. You probably wouldn't like it." I was surprised to hear that, but I think he sized the guy up right away. He said a few things that were unpalatable to Ron. When Ron expressed his disagreement, I remarked that Luang Por teaches that Dharma is never wrong; it may disagree with us, but then we are wrong, not Dharma. "How does he know?" Ron argued. "Maybe that's just his opinion."

Anyhow, I went.

I was in Bangkok for several weeks. Acupuncture really did help my knees, but just as I was ready to leave for the South I got sick. It was only a flu, but when it came on it was similar to the beginnings of hepatitis. That kicked off a chain reaction of thoughts. I'd spent quite a lot of the last two years recuperating from one condition or another, and the thought of continuing to do so was not appealing. Though I knew I had benefited from enduring illness, I now felt that my practice was at a low ebb, largely due to being in poor physical condition and not having much energy to practice. So for the first time, I seriously began to think about disrobing.

During the first difficult years in robes, I often wished I were somewhere else, but I never really thought about disrobing as an option that was open to me; it would have been like leaving the hospital in the middle of surgery. When I was in the U.S., I felt some attraction to what sometimes appeared to be celestial conditions for living and practicing, but I could see through it to perceive many of the problems of lay life. Indeed, before going there I had been experiencing a phase that Ajahn Jun had predicted and warned me about, i.e. attraction to family life, thinking that I'd learned enough to be a good layman and could raise a family in a proper way according to Dharma, etc. But when I actually saw old friends who were married, I was impressed more by their suffering than anything else, and it really knocked that fantasy out of me. Now, however, I realized that if I were to leave, I wouldn't die of grief or guilt. I'd completed the five vassa, I felt that I could take care of myself, and I knew I'd continue to practice wherever I lived. And the trip to the West had shown me that there were teachers and Sanghas to be found outside of the walls of the monastery. It seemed that my practice so far had consisted largely of "hanging in there," and while that had certainly been appropriate up to now and had brought much benefit, perhaps it had reached the point of diminishing returns, and there might be better ways to practice.

It was very sudden and took me by surprise. I realized I would have to give it serious consideration and couldn't just come to a quick decision. I didn't want to discuss it with anyone, partly because it felt like a forbidden subject to talk about, partly because I knew what people would say and that only I could decide this.

I decided I should go ahead with my plan to travel around Thailand, though my enthusiasm was not great, especially since it was hot season by now. First I took a train to Prajuapkirikan province and stayed at a small wat that a monk at Wat Bah Pong had told me about. I'll skip the details and just mention a few salient points at this stage in the story. Ajahn Chah was quite famous by this time (1977). People came from all over Thailand to Wat Bah Pong, and his name was known everywhere. As a disciple of his, I was well-received in the places I travelled to, and when I saw other Wat Bah Pong monks (such as at Wat Suan Moke) I felt that their appearance and conduct were pleasing and worthy of respect, much more so than the general run of monks (which isn't saying much, of course), and usually more than meditation monks from other places, though perhaps I was biased or conditioned to expect certain outward signs. Also there was an especially great difference between the lay people in the Northeast and those anywhere else

I went, and this I think is obvious to anyone who travels around Thailand. The Northeast is poor and can't compare with other areas as far as material offerings go, but lay people there are much more interested in actual practice, probably just because the plague of modernization, technology, material progress, etc. has not yet eaten too far into the substance of life there. At any rate, I began to feel much fondness for the miserable old *Isan* while I was in the South.

As for walking tudong, I set out from Prajuap for Suan Moke; I left in the late afternoon, and kind of liked the walking. But the next day I started earlier. After walking for 10 minutes my robes were soaked with sweat, and all I could think was, anybody who does something like this must be crazy. I was very happy when people offered to put me on buses or trains after that.

After three months of stewing in my juice, the decision to disrobe finally appeared of its own. It clearly seemed the right thing for me to do. Luang Por was in England with Ajahn Sumedho at the time. Of course I would have to wait for him to return. Contemplating the showdown, the moment when I would go to see him in Bangkok and, with Ajahn Sumedho sitting there, tell him that I was going to disrobe, I died 1000 deaths.

However, when I was in Chiengmai, passing the remaining time until Luang Por's return (and leaving open the possibility of a last-moment change of heart), I heard the news that Luang Por had decided to leave Ajahn Sumedho and the others in England. I'm ashamed to say it was a relief to know that I wouldn't have to face Ajahn Sumedho as well as Luang Por, though in the end it turned out more difficult to deal with Luang Por's subtle tactics than if it had just been the matter of brute force that I had expected.

But back to the South for a moment. One of the great subjects of debate in those days was a young monk, formerly at Wat Bah Pong, who was believed by some to have become an Arhat. I was discussing it with the abbot of the monastery in Prajuap, and he just said, "Arhats are really different from ordinary people, but it's very hard to know who's an Arhat. You could be living with one and not know it." He repeated, "You could be living with one and not know it," and afterwards I wondered if he was hinting at something. He was an extremely even-tempered man, and I'd never seen him lose his cool. Who knows? I was never so intrigued by the question of what someone else might have attained; but it is nice to know that hidden away in various little corners throughout Thailand there are practicers who just do their thing and seem to benefit from it.

Luang Por returned just before the beginning of vassa. He was staying at Mae Bow's. With much trepidation I went out there one night, planning to inform him of my decision, then go to Ubon with him to take leave of the Sangha. I wanted to disrobe at Wat Boworn; doing it in Ubon would have been too heavy. I had already spoken to the abbot, who had ordained me as a novice, and had also ordered my pants.

When I arrived, Luang Por was talking to a large group of lay people about his trip to England. His eyes were half-closed as he spoke, and I sat down unnoticed. All I remember of his talk was how he described walking around London in the early morning, seeing people walking their dogs. From the clear picture he drew, I had the feeling that he understood the psychology of people in England very well.

(Luang Por kept a journal on his trip, and it has been printed a few times. It was his first plane trip, and Ajahn Sumedho had long suspected that Luang Por was afraid to fly. He used to ask questions like "Are there toilets on the airplanes?" as if he were seeking an excuse not to fly. Then on his very first flight, the plane had some mechanical trouble, and there was an announcement that everyone should put on their life vests. The Thai people on the plane came to Luang Por for blessing and protection, and according to Ajahn Sumedho, Luang Por just figured, so this is it, this is what happens when you fly).

He finished talking, opened his eyes, and noticed me. After the introductory insults, he asked me where I was going to spend vassa. I just answered that I had to consult with him. Then he asked me what I wanted to do in the future. Did I want to go tudong or live in solitude, did I want to teach, did I want to become a scholar … ? I again answered that I had to consult with him. It felt like a stage production: I imagined that he knew what was on my mind, maybe everyone in the room knew, yet he was going through this act with me.

Finally the lay people left. I sat alone with Luang Por and one

115

other Thai monk. He said, OK, what are you going to do? and I told him that I'd come to the decision to disrobe.

Heavy silence.

Then he asked what it was that had led me to this. I went through my well-rehearsed litany: practice was mostly a matter of endurance, I didn't feel that my meditation was developing, the climate, illness, and the ascetic way of life seemed to be big obstacles, and after long consideration I really thought a change of life-style would be beneficial.

He seemed neither impressed with my line of reasoning nor pleased with my conclusion. He didn't try to argue with me. He just said, "You went tudong and this is what you bring me." And then in English, "Thank you very much." He got up and said it was time to go to sleep, leaving me sitting there feeling like I'd been kicked in the groin.

The next day he didn't say anything to me about it, and in the evening the lay people put us on the train for Ubon. They insisted on first class berths for us, though Luang Por said "Put Varapanyo in third class. He likes third class." I guess it was a sign that he still cared. He went to sleep soon after the train left, so there was no discussion.

The next morning at the Warin station, it looked like half the people in Ubon had turned out to greet him. A large number of monks were there, and we went pindapat in town, then to Wat Bah Pong for the meal. I rode in a truck with the farang monks from Bung Wai, but didn't answer their questions about where I was spending vassa, only saying that I would speak to the Sangha at Bung Wai about it soon. I did tell Ajahn Pabhakaro, with whom I had ordained, now the new abbot of Wat Bung Wai. He didn't have much to say because he was so surprised, though he did grill me a few days later. After the meal we went back to Bung Wai.

I announced my decision to the Sangha. Generally they seemed to respect it. I was the senior farang at the time, for one thing, and I'd kept my half of the five vassa bargain. After a few days there I went to Wat Bah Pong to take final leave of Luang Por, or so I thought. At this point my mind was made up, and second thoughts weren't bothering me. I really felt like I'd had enough.

I went to see Luang Por before pindapat. He was upstairs when

I got to his kuti. A familiar looking young monk was waiting there. He asked me if I remembered him. It was Gun Ha, the reputed Arhat. He just struck me as being the same pleasant, soft-spoken fellow I'd known a few years ago. He too asked me where I was. going to spend vassa, and I dodged the question once more by saying that I had to speak with Luang Por first. I thought, he's supposed to be able to read minds, why is he asking me?

Once years before, while sitting with Luang Por at his kuti, I had what seemed like a little insight into the subject of reading minds. A GI named Jerry was visiting from the Ubon base. He'd come a few times, and on this occasion we'd gone to see Luang Por so Jerry could take a picture of him (which was quite comical in itself, Luang Por struggling so hard to put on a serious face as Thais are supposed to do for a picture). Then Luang Por started asking Jerry questions, which soon revealed the various worries, burdens etc. that plagued him. At the time Luang Por had a caged squirrel at his kuti, which somebody had brought to him. I watched the squirrel jumping around in its cage, unable to go anywhere but also unable to be still. Then I looked at Jerry, who was obviously squirming as Luang Por spoke to him. It seemed to me that Luang Por probably saw all of us like that; our states of mind would be as clear to him as the squirrel's condition was to me right then. Perhaps there is a lot more to psychic powers than this, but it demystified the subject for me somewhat and made me think that it's probably mostly a matter of sensitivity, i.e. awareness. Luang Por has said that just as an adult can understand children because he's experienced what they are now experiencing, so someone who's clearly seen and transcended the patterns of thoughts and emotions can understand them in other people, and that facial expressions and physical gestures reveal states of mind to such a person.

I mentioned this episode to a visiting Western woman who said, "I hope Luang Por doesn't see *me* like that (i.e. like the squirrel)." I said that I was afraid that he sees us all that way, to which she answered, "Well, that's just tough on Luang Por."

He came downstairs. Even before he sat down, he growled at me, in Lao, "What are you going to do?" Whenever he spoke to me in Lao in that tone I knew I was in for a hard time. I said that I'd come to take leave; I was going back to Bangkok to disrobe, as I'd explained before. "How about staying for one more vassa?" he asked. No, I'd made up my mind and there didn't seem to be any point to it. He said that he thought I should stay at least another three months, and then if I still wanted to disrobe, there wouldn't be any doubt remaining, and I could leave knowing I wasn't making a mistake. I answered that I really had to disrobe. "What do you mean, you 'have to' disrobe? You haven't 'stabbed any assholes,' have you?" Meaning that as long as I hadn't done something of that order, I couldn't say that I "had to" disrobe. It went back and forth for a while, and I began to see my whole neatly constructed scheme of things dissolving right before my eyes. It had all seemed so solid and real, and now he was making magic tricks with it. It was a little frightening, but I could see it from his point of view, so I finally said that I would think about it. Still in the same gruff Lao, he said, I really care about you, that's why I'm saying this.

I went back to my kuti and decided to forget about eating. I threw the I Ching, something I wasn't in the habit of doing, and it basically said to consider cautiously before acting, or that the time wasn't right. Then when I took a rest at midday I dreamed that I was at the tailor shop and my pants didn't fit. Luang Por had put me in quite a state of turmoil, and that afternoon I went to tell him that I'd sign on for three more months. He said I should go to Bung Wai and practice as I wished (my knees were still fragile and couldn't keep up with the full schedule of group practice). After we finished discussing it, I got up to go, and he mischievously said, you won't disrobe, you'll stay another vassa and get over it. "Three more months," I said.

Back at Bung Wai, I worked out the details with Ajahn Pabhakaro. He would sit in the abbot's seat, I would do my own practice, but I would teach Vinaya after evening chanting. I had to make a new announcement to the Sangha, then get to Bangkok to undo my various arrangements, and come back right away for the beginning of vassa.

The Northeast was having one of its periodic droughts, it was very hot, and after two weeks I was in the same old rut. I had said I would put the decision-making process on the shelf for the three months, but it had already fallen off the shelf; nothing had changed, and I really wanted to pack it in. I threw the I Ching again and it said

I could go. So when one young bhikkhu and a visiting Indian monk from Buriram province wanted to go see Luang Por, I offered to go along to translate for them, thinking (once again) that I would take leave of Luang Por.

The farang monk had a doubt concerning a possible *Sanghadisesa* offence from many months before. At the time he had consulted Ajahn Sumedho who told him it wasn't an offense. But the doubts crept up on him. When he explained it to Luang Por, Luang Por listened and just said, let go of it; it's the past. The monk thought maybe Luang Por hadn't understood the details of what he was telling him, but Luang Por just kept telling him to drop it, the past is over and done with. He saw that the monk had difficulty accepting this—it was certainly different from the way Luang Por usually reacted to this issue—so he told us that when he was a new monk he had many similar worries. When he used things belonging to the Sangha, he thought maybe he was *Parajika* for stealing; sometimes he thought that maybe he wasn't really a bhikkhu, since his Upajjhaya didn't keep the Vinaya properly (i.e. if ordination is given by one whose bhikkhuhood is not valid, then the ordination is likewise not valid. Minor infractions are not sufficient to invalidate bhikkhuhood). He had had many such doubts, but finally he got wise to the doubting process itself and let go of it.

Next came Ajanyo, the "Pra Kack" ("Indian monk"—"kack" often has a somewhat derogatory flavor; it refers to all those of Indian and Arabian origin. A Thai proverb says, "If you meet a snake and a kack, beat the kack first.") He was very unhappy with the way things were being done at Bung Wai. He was an extreme case of chronic faultfinding, and none of us took him very seriously, but Ajahn Pabhakaro agreed to let him come to see Luang Por. Luang Por spoke very politely and explained things very patiently for him. He calmed down momentarily, but the next week he went with Ajahn Pabhakaro to complain to Luang Por again. When Ajahn Pabhakaro recounted that meeting he said that Luang Por was once again very tolerant and polite, though firm (as he was the first time), and that Luang Por showed real humility towards somebody who had none.

Finally it was my turn. I told Luang Por that it wasn't working out and I was perfectly sure that I wanted to disrobe. He said, fine; just wait until vassa is over. I replied that I just felt like I was wasting time. "Wasting time," he said. "I waste a lot of time. I'm an old man, I'm 60 years old; I'm always wasting time." I said that I felt like I was taking the alms of the lay people in bad faith, that I was only half a person because my heart wasn't in it. "This I have to see," he said, "half a person. I'll put an ad in the newspaper so people can come to see the farang monk who's only half a person."

He wouldn't budge. I did the three prostrations and left. As I approached the eating hall, I saw one of the farang, and I said, "I'm gonna get a lawyer." It seemed like the only way to deal with the guy.

Ordaining and disrobing were serious issues with Ajahn Chah, so I suppose I should have known that he wouldn't easily let me go. Most temples in Thailand will ordain people instantly, for as long or short a period as they wish. Luang Por had stopped the temporary ordinations for a while, because he really believed that a person should do a minimum of five years, and not just on his own, but under the guidance of a teacher. This wasn't his own invention, it is the Buddha's way as recorded in the Vinaya. But after refusing temporary ordinations for a while, he began to accept them again, I think because he knew that they would ordain anyhow and end up in a village or city wat where they could learn very little, and practice even less. However, he still felt that people who had come and ordained with faith and the desire to escape from suffering should not give up easily, and preferably should remain in robes forever. He saw a vast difference between monks' life and lay life.

The reactions of most Thai monks when they heard about me were predictable. One monk told someone else to tell me that he was never going to disrobe. "I'm very happy for him," I said. When I had been in Chiengmai before seeing Luang Por, I discussed it with the abbot at Doy Puey, Ajahn Pyrote. I told him that I thought I could further my practice in a new situation. He said, "Don't tell me you're disrobing to practice. If you admit that you want to disrobe to have a good time, that's OK, but don't try to tell me that you want to practice ... If I were to disrobe today, I'd get married tomorrow." He'd been a monk for 19 years, and it isn't unusual for a senior monk to disrobe and get married tomorrow. In Thailand there's little hope for a layperson to practice as intensely as a monk, so such opinions are understandable. Even for Luang Por, it was difficult to grasp. He asked me, do you want to become rich? Do you want to get married? When I replied in the negative to all such questions, he asked, so why do you want to disrobe? Again, I could understand his scepticism. I'd seen many Thai monks disrobe, and none of them looked very inspiring when they came around to visit as laymen. And the ones who came to visit were probably in much better shape than the ones who didn't come.

Ajahn Pyrote said, "Being a monk is pretty good. We don't have to work, and they bring us food. If they'd let us have wives it would be perfect ... But for a lot of people, being ordained is like being in a hospital. No matter how nice the conditions are, nobody wants to stay in a hospital all their life."

Did the old man have me foiled? I was pretty unhappy, and there didn't seem to be any way out. I went back to Bung Wai and simmered for a while. Early one morning, staying up on Wun Pra, I finally calmed down a little, and I realized that if I wanted to pull this off, I couldn't be in an angry state of mind; I needed all the clarity I could muster. I sat down and wrote a respectful, thoughtful letter to Luang Por, and sent it with the next person going to Wat Bah Pong. A few days later some Bung Wai monks went to a meal in town with Luang Por, and he sent word back: he wasn't going to hold me there against my will.

I completed the section of the Vinaya I had been reading to the monks, and once more went to take leave of Luang Por. When I went to see him, he innocently asked, what's doing? You're going to stay for the rest of vassa, right? But I held my ground and reminded him that he'd said I could go. Then he said that he was coming to Bung Wai in a few days and I could take formal leave of him then. So he eluded me once more, but the end was in sight.

For two nights at Bung Wai I hung around the sala with my tray of incense and candles, but he talked late into the night and I didn't get a chance to do the ceremony. Finally he said we could all "tam wat" him in the morning before he left.

The Last Breakfast finally arrived. As we ate in silence, he called my name. "When you go to Wat Boworn, what are you going to tell the Somdet your reason is for disrobing in the middle of vassa?" I said that I would tell him what had happened, that Luang Por

121

suggested trying another three months but it just wasn't working out. "Having trouble breathing," Luang Por said. We went back to eating.

"Varapanyo!"

"Krup."

"When you go to Bangkok and are disrobed, take a picture and send it to us."

"Krup."

"Take a picture with a 'partner.'" This brought loud laughter from the gallery, perhaps a few monks choking on their food, and then he let us finish the meal in peace.

We did the ceremony of asking forgiveness for misdeeds of body, speech and mind. He very gently said how sorry he was to see me go, "like losing one arm." Then he told me to dump all my suffering in the sea, to keep what was good and get rid of what was no good. As he walked towards the car, he turned around and stuck out his hand. "Shake hands," he said. "We never shook hands." I guess he'd learned that in England.

Afterwards, I was able to reflect on all of this, and I saw how he gave me a hard time right up to the end, but then when he let me go, he gave his blessing. I think he was being thorough on all counts.

I said good-bye to the Sangha that night, telling them I hoped they could stay there and get enlightened and not have to leave as I was doing. Indeed, I felt that I *had* to leave as much as or more than I wanted to leave. The next night I took the train to Bangkok. I stopped off at Mae Bow's, where everyone already knew, Luang Por having been there recently for the Queen's birthday party. I had felt a little uneasy about telling the lay people who had supported me so faithfully, but they were very tolerant. Mae Bow said she had asked Luang Por, couldn't I be convinced to change my mind, but Luang Por told her it was too late, I was a goner. Then she told me of the Thai maxim that there are three things that can't be stopped: someone who has to go to the toilet, a woman who's about to give birth, and a monk who wants to disrobe.

Then on to Wat Boworn where I saw the Somdet, who told me to gather a few monks and do it at the foreign monks' quarters. It was a much simpler procedure than ordination. I recited the formula, in Pali and Thai: "Venerable sirs, I now leave the training;

you should know me as a layman." When I changed into pants and shirt, it didn't feel at all strange. I took the five precepts and called it a night.

I had been with an Australian monk in Chonburi when I came to the decision to disrobe, and I discussed it with him. He said, "Sometimes I think I want to disrobe, and I think, what would I do? I'd put on pants and walk down the street ... maybe I'd eat a bowl of 'guey tio' (noodle soup) ... then what would I do?" So the next morning, I put on pants and walked down the street. I ate a plate of fried rice instead. It felt wonderful not to be stuffed and sleepy after eating. I hung around Bangkok for two weeks, getting acupuncture and arranging a plane ticket, and then I left for California, where an old friend had a place to live and some work for me, and a Zen Sangha to meet. I wasn't at all interested in staying in Thailand anymore. Of course I didn't know what to expect "out there," but I felt some confidence due to the training I'd had. I knew I'd continue to meditate under any circumstances, and I thought that the foundation Luang Por had given me would help me keep on the right track.

Ajahn Chah on his visit to the U.S. in 1979.

VIII

"In order to understand the true nature of reality, there is no better method than developing intense, fervent devotion towards the Guru and relying on him completely."

(Summer 1989)

It was September 1977 when I disrobed, and I didn't see Luang Por Chah until May 1979 for a brief though unique time, and then again until December 1981, shortly after his operation. So obviously there is much that others could tell about that period. I know that just by having dropped by his kuti or going pindapat with him on numerable occasions I came away with many interesting stories, points of Dharma, or whole desanas that I could just as easily have missed. On his trip to the U.S. alone, a book could have been created from the teachings he gave, many of which were unique due to the situation. Someday I'm sure an "official" biography will be compiled; may others contribute.

My experiences in lay life are not important here, except for perhaps the facts that my reverence for Ajahn Chah continued to grow, I continued to practice, and I felt that my training at Wat Bah Pong was the basis which enabled me to practice other forms of Buddhism. There was nobody to make a deal with except myself this time, but I had it in mind that I should probably undertake another five year plan, i.e. endure the ups and downs without either running right back to the monastery or committing myself to something like a career, marriage, etc.

When I was a monk I often got letters from a friend at home who was struggling to practice as a layman, praising me for my goodness, dedication, and other qualities which I was sure I didn't possess. But after disrobing and getting out there in the trenches, I too began to think of the monks with great reverence, not necessarily for their individual virtues, but for leading a pure way of life, creating a moral force in the world and offering inspiration and a good example for others.

I saw Jack Kornfield occasionally, and we kept in touch because we both had teachings of Ajahn Chah that we had translated, and Jack was eager to get something published. He also hoped to have Luang Por come to the U.S. In May of 1979 I got a telegram from Jack saying that Luang Por would soon be arriving in Seattle with Ajahn Pabhakaro. Jack had arranged for me to travel as their attendant, so I flew to Seattle the day before their arrival.

The next night I went to the airport with the Kappels (Pabhakaro's family), feeling a mixture of joy, devotion, and trepidation. A group of local vipassana practicers met us there. The flight came in and all the passengers walked out into the arrival area, but no Luang Por. Then a few minutes later he appeared, moving at his own pace. I went up to him and kneeled down, and he asked, in Lao, "Have you disrobed yet?" I didn't know what to say to that. He repeated it, then said he was going to the toilet. Ajahn Pabhakaro and I escorted him. When he got inside his serious face disappeared and he started laughing hysterically, pointing at me and laughing.

The others welcomed him with flowers and folded palms, and then it was agreed that we would all go back to the Kappels' house for a brief get-together. Tea was served, he talked with them a little, and we began to make a schedule for invitations to meals, a public talk, and meditation instruction. It was getting late and they had flown from Boston, so the people left and we went upstairs to prepare Luang Por's quarters. He sat in a chair and watched us, and soon he called me over. I went and sat at his feet, and he immediately started giving me the business. In his gruffest Lao he asked me what I was doing with myself, not waiting for the answers which I struggled to produce with my unpracticed tongue, but just ridiculing me. "Come back to the forest and do it like we do it. Get away from women and all this confusion … "

The days to come were like that. I tried to tell him that I hadn't abandoned practice and that I'd been studying with a Zen teacher; he would keep asking me what Zen was about and then make fun of my answers. He told me I should keep the eight precepts, which wasn't so enticing to me, and he told the Kappels not to feed me in the PM. All in all, he was being as cantankerous as anyone could possibly be. Gone from my perceptions was the wise, compassionate and humorous master I thought I once knew, and I honestly began to wonder if this was all there was to Ajahn Chah, a difficult, narrow-minded "Hinayanist." Had I really lived with this guy for all those years? Then I remembered that I was supposed to be writing a book about him, but at that point all I could think of was that I wanted to get away from him.

After a few days we went to the Kappels' home in Steven's Pass, outside of Seattle, a large cabin by a river in a quiet wooded area. He was still being unbearable, so I called the vipassana people in Seattle and invited them to come out and offer food one day, thinking I could escape with them and at least get a few days' respite.

One evening when the Kappels were out we lit a fire and sat around drinking tea. Once again he asked, "What does Zen teach?" I said that one's own enlightenment was not considered to be the end, because one had to liberate others as well. "The Bodhisattva," he said, and then went on to give a very accurate description of the Bodhisattva ideal. He used one simile that I'd heard in other quarters. The Arhat, he said, is like someone who's finished high school, while the Bodhisattva has gone on to get a doctorate. With a high school education one can manage very well. He can't get the fame and high position of a Ph.D., but he's satisfied with what he has. "Whoever is beyond doubt and can remain in the world, fine," he said, meaning the Bodhisattva.

Gone all of a sudden was the cantankerousness. He was Luang Por again, pulling rabbits out of the hat, giving his unique teachings and making me laugh. Even Ajahn Pabhakaro loosened up a bit. Though we used to be partners in crime in the old days, he was now an abbot and was playing it straight, and had been kicking me after Luang Por had knocked me down.

What an actor! I had fallen for it completely. I think many others have had this experience of "Luang Por" vanishing and a hostile old man taking his place. One bhikkhu told me that the first time he recited the Patimokkha at Wat Bah Pong, as soon as he started fumbling Luang Por did his usual routine: pulling on his robe from behind, making jokes, starting conversations with the monks sitting near him, thereby destroying concentration and memory as well as the last shreds of self-esteem. The monk said that at that point, "That wasn't Luang Por anymore, it was just some fat old man pulling on my robe." One Thai monk once told me how difficult it was to sit in the eating hall after the meal. It wasn't part of the daily routine, but occasionally Luang Por would keep us there as he talked with a layman or made jokes with the senior monks. Of course he was aware of everyone's restlessness but he acted very innocent, as if he had forgotten we were there. "When he makes us sit there like that, he's not Luang Por to me, I only feel aversion." After I'd seen teachers in the West who generally didn't tell people anything disagreeable, I began to think that it's an extremely compassionate teacher who's willing to make people hate him.

So now in all earnestness he asked me about what I'd been doing, how I viewed things in the world, and I got to ask him questions based on my study of Mahayana, working with the dying, and observations of Buddhadharma being transplanted in Western society.

Though he had never read Mahayana texts, except maybe for the Altar Sutra of the Sixth Patriarch, his understanding of Mahayana principles was pretty keen, to say the least. It made me wonder what kind of things we might have heard from him if we had asked the right questions over the years. On working with the dying, which was becoming popular at the time of his visit, he said that most of the benefit was to be found by those who visited the dying, by contemplating the truths of sickness and death, rather than by those we might visit and try to help. I had come to have strong doubts, thinking that by trying to comfort dying people we might interfere with the ego-dissolution process which could give people real insight. Also the glorious accounts of those who described the bliss and peacefulness that people realized in their final moments, even though they had been resistant and fearful through most of the dying process, didn't seem to accord with the law of karma. Luang Por said that it was unlikely that we could affect the state of mind of a dying person very much, either positively or adversely. He took his cane and poked me in the chest and said, if this were a red hot iron and I were poking you with it, and then I held out a piece of candy with my other hand, how much could the candy distract you? He also said that it was very difficult to know what people were experiencing at death by observing them. I told him how people described the transformations that came over the dying, how they went out smiling peacefully. He said, "When pigs are taken to be slaughtered, they too are smiling up to the last moment. Can we say that the pigs are all going to Nirvana?"

He emphasized that of course we should treat dying people with love and compassion and look after them as best we can, but that if we don't turn it inward to contemplate our own inevitable death, there is little real benefit for us. The theme of immanent death was to be one he returned to over and over as the trip progressed.

I looked back on this episode later on and wondered if he had been testing me by acting so ornery. When faced with his criticism, ridicule, and negativity, I had felt like sticking to my guns, i.e. my practice as a layman. It also helped sever the remaining strands of longing for monk's life. Maybe he was reflecting my divided mind and forcing me to cut through it. This was what my Zen teacher immediately said when I told him about all this afterwards.

He was also very tired, and for the first week or so slept a lot. Of course I was aware that he rarely had a chance for a real rest in Thailand, but he seemed so totally exhausted that I thought maybe he was over the hill and just didn't have the strength to teach people anymore. He seemed content to sit around at night and share his Dharma with the two of us. Some nights he would tell us to turn on the TV and would sit there in silence, watching moronic programs and commercials in a language he couldn't understand at all. But before long he was to be teaching with enthusiasm, probably because he saw that there were people who were sincerely interested, and also I think because his body hadn't lost all of its once-amazing recuperative powers, and the rest he got really helped him. Then I began to see that as he watched TV and observed people on our trips around the area, he was gaining knowledge of Western life. Sometimes he pointed out specific things to illustrate his teaching, other times he would just make general statements like "Westerners are so pitiful" or "They really like to try out everything in this society."

We were given the use of a neighboring house for a few days, and one night I sat alone with Luang Por as Ajahn Pabhakaro visited with his family. From his armchair he said "Let's sit in samadhi." I sat on the floor beside him, not knowing if he was awake or asleep; there didn't seem to be much energy emanating from him. Finally he stirred, and we started talking. He often began conversations with "What do you think, Varapanyo?" followed by something like "How can we spread Buddhism here?" He said that he hadn't been overly impressed with the few teachers he'd seen in the West, for although they taught people how to practice meditation techniques, they hadn't challenged people ("stabbed their hearts" I think he said), hadn't gotten down to the root of things. I am reminded of Sasaki Roshi who has said that people here like Zen meditation but are not yet interested in Mahayana Zen, and when asked what he thought of Zen in the West, said that as far as he could see, Zen hadn't yet come to the West.

I told him that one of the ideas that some teachers gave students was that since everything is empty, there weren't really such things as attachment and suffering. You can't do it that way, Luang Por said, you have to use the conventions. I said that many people contend that since the mind is inherently pure, since we all have Buddha nature, it's not necessary to practice. His answer was, "You have something clean, like this tray. I come and drop some shit on it. Will you say 'This tray is originally clean, so I don't have to do anything to clean it now'?" On another occasion I told him how some people think they're happy, so they don't want to practice. He said, if a child won't go to school but tells his parents, "It's OK, I'm fine like this," is that right? Then there are those who say that suffering is Dharma, therefore it's good, so we should "honor" it, not try to end it. He said, "Right. I tell them, don't let go of it, just hold on to it as long as you can and see what it feels like." He admitted that it was true that Nirvana and Samsara are inseparable, like the palm and the back of the hand, but that one has to turn the hand over. Finally he said that if people present all these invincible arguments and don't want to be convinced of the truth, "just let them be like that. Where will they get to?" i.e. such people have to see it for themselves.

He said that when he met the vipassana teacher, Munindra, he offered some advice on teaching. In order to get to the heart of the matter without frightening people away, it's necessary to loosen them up a bit. Don't call it Buddhism—it's just Satya Dharma, truth. Tell them, "This isn't my opinion," "Please pardon me for speaking like this," etc. Talk of things that are relevant to people, but don't point out faults too directly. For example, drinking: you can say, if "someone" drinks it may give them some pleasure, but ... or, "I used to do such things until I saw the harm in them." Of course this wasn't only a problem in teaching Westerners. He mentioned on several occasions how it was difficult to teach people in Thailand as well, and often would say "I don't know who to talk to anymore." Indeed, as time went on he seemed to gain enthusiasm for teaching Westerners, saying once again how in Thailand he felt like a chained monkey that people came to see for entertainment value. Also he repeated his simile of Buddhism in Thailand as a big old tree, which may look majestic but can only give small, sour fruits. Buddhism in the West he saw as a sapling, not yet able to bear fruit but having potential.

I asked him once more about the Bodhisattva ideal. The Vimalakirti Sutra says something like, "Though beyond attachment, the Bodhisattva does not cut off the streams of passion so as to remain in the world for the benefit of sentient beings." Luang Por said, that's not talking about the mind itself, but the function of the mind. It's like asking, "Do you want this?"

"No."

"Do you like it?"

"Yes."

"Do you want it?"

"No."

"Is it beautiful?"

"Yes."

"So do you want it?"

"No."

But he *really* doesn't want it, he's not merely talking, Luang Por added.

When I said that the Bodhisattva concept was profound, he said,

131

"Don't think like that. It is your own thinking that is shallow or deep, long or short. There's not so much to it, but you get caught in your doubting mind."

Should we get everyone else to Nirvana first? "The Buddha didn't leave us after his enlightenment, but stayed to help others gain liberation. But we can do only so much and that's enough. If we save all beings in the world now, the next Buddha won't have a world to be born into." When I asked Ajahn Chah if he was going to return to teach in his next life, he said "No, I'm tired. One life of teaching is enough." He sounded like he meant it.

Being outside of the usual setting of the monastery and Thai society, we didn't have to observe all the usual formalities, which was another thing that made this time special. He often used the informal first person pronoun with me, and I wondered if he sometimes saw Varapanyo in his robes as I sat before him.

I made the arrangements with the Seattle people, and one morning when I was in charge of the kitchen, the Kappels having gone out for the day, they came out to offer food. Luang Por had asked, who's the cook today ("kitchen mother"), and when I said that I was, he said with cynicism and astonishment, "You can cook?" I think it was difficult for him to conceive of me doing such worldly things.

I wasn't aware of it at the time, but that morning Luang Por was feeling quite discouraged. The night before he'd been shown some girlie magazines, and he felt great pity mixed with hopelessness to see such degradation, which indicated deep ignorance. As he sat on the lawn with Ajahn Pabhakaro that morning, he was saying that maybe they should just forget about the rest of the trip and go back home; how could such people be taught? Then these young Westerners showed up. They had come to offer food and hear teaching. It brightened his outlook considerably, and from that point he began to teach with real enthusiasm.

The night I had been alone with him, he said that on this trip he was only going to tell people to sit and do formal meditation practice. I told him that that was what most teachers had been doing. But when he actually started talking to people, the message was much different.

After the meal we meditated together, and then he answered

questions. I don't remember the questions as much as the detailed answers. Basically he was teaching about right understanding. He said that the approach many people had to meditation was like a thief who after he gets caught hires a clever lawyer to get him out of trouble. Once he is out, he starts stealing again. Luang Por also compared it to a boxer who gets beaten up, nurses his wounds, and then goes to fight again, which only brings him fresh wounds. And this cycle goes on endlessly. The purpose of meditation is more than just calming ourselves from time to time, getting ourselves out of trouble, but seeing and uprooting the causes which produce trouble and make us not calm to begin with.

He was aware of the way people went from teacher to teacher, practice to practice, and he repeatedly told people that wisdom was not to be gained by getting a lot of knowledge or dabbling in different ways of meditation, but by understanding the essential points and then practicing them. He told a story of a wanderer in the Buddha's time. He would hear about a teacher, go to see him, and begin to practice his way, and would then hear of another teacher somewhere else. He'd find that teacher and follow him, until somebody told him of some other teacher who was supposed to be very great, so off he'd go again. Finally he ended up at Buddha's place, and explained that he was getting confused and tired from all of this. The Buddha told him, "Forget about what has passed, don't anticipate anything in the future, but now contemplate what is arising and passing away in the present moment." Through doing this, the wanderer made an end of doubt.

Luang Por also emphasized patience. One of the people asked him about Stream Entry, the first level of enlightenment. He answered that of course one practices to experience realizations such as Stream Entry ("falling into the stream" in Thai), but it takes perseverance. If such things were easy, everyone would be doing them. He said, "I started going to the temple when I was eight years old, I've been a monk for over 40 years. You farang want to meditate for a night or two and go straight to Nirvana ... You don't just sit down and fall right into the stream, you can't get someone to blow on your head and make you enlightened."

He seemed to get a kick out of hearing bits of Mahayana Sutras that I would occasionally translate for him, often saying that they

133

were expressions of deep wisdom, but sometimes he would turn them around and challenge me, reminding me not to be satisfied with conceptual knowledge. Once when I said that according to Mahayana, the Arhat has only travelled half the path, he asked, "Has anyone ever travelled the whole path?" When I said that Sariputta, the embodiment of wisdom in the Pali Scriptures, became the fool in many Mahayana texts, he said "The people who read these things are the real fools." Needless to say, I'm sure he wasn't denigrating the Sutras, only poking those who merely grasp the words without experiencing the deep meaning. Talking about the Diamond Sutra, I said "This Sutra says, 'He who sees all forms as unreal sees the Tathagata,'" which prompted him to look down at me very fiercely and say "Yeah, is that so?" More than once he asked me if I knew who wrote these Sutras. Well, they say the Buddha did. "Do you know who Buddha is?" he demanded. I had to keep my mouth shut.

So by this time I was having fun and didn't want to escape from him anymore. The people went back to Seattle without me. We spent a few more days in Steven's Pass, eating huge meals, taking walks, occasionally sitting in meditation together, chatting in the evening. He really seemed to be interested in my experience as a layman and my point of view on things. He began to say that I was really difficult to figure out, that I was neither a monk nor a layman ("he looks like a layman but he doesn't think like a layman; he thinks like a monk but he's not a monk"). He said it was OK to be in such an in-between state for the time being—provided I kept on shaving my head. "Don't be in a hurry to get rid of your defilements," he once told me. I asked why, and he said that I should patiently get to know suffering and its causes well, then I could abandon them thoroughly, just as it's better for your digestion if you chew your food slowly and thoroughly.

When we went back to Seattle, there was a pretty full schedule planned, part of which was a trip to Vancouver. He was certainly more energetic than when he had arrived, but one of the people who had come out to Steven's Pass suggested that he see a Chinese doctor in Seattle. We went, not expecting much, but he gave Luang Por some herbs which soon turned him into a bundle of dynamite.

He gave one public talk in Seattle, at the Quaker Center. It was mostly about Sila. He started right out by scolding everyone in a kindly way, sort of like, "Now you know you shouldn't be doing all these things you do." I was a little surprised by it, and it certainly wasn't as interesting or exciting as a talk about meditation, emptiness, etc., but as time went by and I saw him returning to this over and over, I began to appreciate it. And in the months and years to follow, I saw more and more how accurate he was. I think that was when he began telling people to beware of meditation teachers. In subsequent talks and conversations, he went into a lot of detail on this subject. He saw a great difference between merely being able to practice meditation and giving the techniques to people on the one hand, and incorporating the practice into your whole life so that one's being *is* Dharma. He felt that those who were not really liberated from their cravings would naturally teach people according to their opinions, and would be very indulgent with their students' habits and desires.

There were questions and answers, then the Mindful Way film (made by the BBC) about Wat Bah Pong was shown. After that, as we prepared to leave, a few people came up to him to ask some more questions. Someone said that as lay people, we can't maintain the kind of separation of the sexes that monks and nuns have, we are forced to deal with the opposite sex. Luang Por answered that there should be friendliness and loving kindness, but it should be based on Dharma, not on desire. He also said that with monastic discipline, by having some distance between the sexes, we were able to have genuine love and respect. Some others asked him about various aspects of the five precepts. He gave very direct and unambiguous answers, such as I hadn't yet heard on the subject. The precepts on sexual misconduct and intoxicants are the subject of much confusion, and often vaguely interpreted. Many people feel that taking intoxicants is OK if not done to the point of intoxication (whatever that may mean). Luang Por answered that if someone is a chronic thief, you don't put temptation in his way. Intoxicants are by nature inducive to heedlessness, so why use them even a little? On sexual conduct and misconduct, he said that if one was able to do it, celibacy is best for a practicer; but if not, one should simply be content with one's partner. "You've got to think, one wife or one husband is more than you can eat, so why do you need many partners?" (We chose not to translate this in its entirety, however).

Luang Por was invited for meals at the house where the local vipassana group met, and led meditations and gave talks there. We also went there one evening for a meditation and a good session of questions and answers. He compared samatha (calm) meditation to putting a chicken in a cage. Within the cage the chicken doesn't stay still or lie down and die. It moves around, but its movement is limited, it can be controlled and observed. He suggested doing meditation on the body if the mind becomes still. If there is a lot of thinking, you can deal with it in various ways, e.g. *kasina* meditation, where you fix your attention on a colored disc or a candle flame until you see it even when you close your eyes. Expand it and contract it, burn up everything with it.

Or you can simply let thinking be, just know it. You sit and it goes off to someone's house—ask it "What did you bring back?" Know that it is impermanent. It isn't your self. When will it ever be self? How long will you have to wait before it can be self? You don't have to know a lot, he said, just observe what is right here until dispassion arises and you can let go of the five aggregates. That's the point of it all.

Someone asked, what is the true seat of the soul? Seeing that there is no soul (self), he answered. There was a question about dealing with lust. Could one concentrate on the energy in the body and see through it that way, or use the energy for awakening? Luang Por just advised letting go of it, not trying to grab it for any reason. The energy of dispassion, he said, is greater than the energy of passion.

Then he gave a little summary. Our life is just an assembly of the elements. We use conventions to describe things, but we get attached to the conventions and take them to be something real. For example, people and things are given names. We could go back to the beginning, before the names are given, and call men women and women men—what would be the difference? But now we are attached to names and concepts, so we have the war of the sexes and other wars as well. Meditation is for seeing through all of this; then we can reach the unconditioned and be at peace, not at war.

Some Thai people had invited Luang Por to Vancouver, so we drove there and stayed for two nights. He gave public talks at a university and on both nights people came back to the apartment where we were staying and he spoke to them until 11 or 12. After they left he spoke to us until 3 AM. The Chinese medicine was clearly doing something for him. Not only was he extremely energetic, but those late sessions were some of the most incredible Dharma I ever heard from him. For much of the time he had his eyes half closed, and he wasn't talking to anyone in particular; it was more like he was revealing his stream of awareness. The second night in particular I had hoped to ask him about the Lotus Sutra, in which Buddha reveals the ultimate meaning and purpose of his teaching and appearance in the world. But as Luang Por talked, he was somehow answering my questions; in a way it felt like the drama of the sutra was being re-enacted. He kept on saying, "I don't know who to talk to about it." He said, "We talk about things to be developed and things to give up, but there's nothing to develop, nothing to give up." The way he spoke, it wasn't exactly clear whether he was referring to himself or just generally speaking about the viewpoint of ultimate truth, but he certainly seemed to know what he was talking about. He mentioned the Arhat, and said "The Arhat is really different from ordinary people"—then he coyly added, "Of course we don't see Arhats nowadays, but I'm going by what it says in the books"—and he said that the things that seem true or valuable to us are false and worthless to an Arhat. Trying to interest an Arhat in worldly things would be like offering lead in exchange for gold. We think, here is a whole pile of lead, why wouldn't he want to trade his piece of gold which is so much smaller?

He also returned to the theme of teaching people, how you had to find skillful means to get around their pride, make them think that they have understood things on their own and praise them for it, as if the teacher had nothing to do with it. He talked about a layman who liked to fish. One day he told the man, "I really feel strange today. I had a dream last night that I was a fish, I swallowed a hook and I was dying in agony … " The layman started thinking about it, and eventually gave up fishing. Then Luang Por would praise him, saying, "This layman saw the truth by himself, he gave up wrong action and practices virtue through his own wisdom, he didn't need a teacher." These are the lengths you have to go to to reach people,

137

he told us. And some people we just can't teach. "I search for some Dharma to give them, but there's nothing there. I don't know what it is—maybe just the karma of that person." And he said he wasn't interested in arguing with people who had little understanding. "It's like a rich man contending with a pauper." Actually, he was sensitive enough that he usually was able to disarm those whom others might have argued with. One simple example of this was when some GI's came to Wat Bah Pong, and as we sat at Luang Por's kuti, one of them slapped mosquitoes. When I told him that we don't kill any creatures in the wat, he was surprised and said, well, they're only mosquitoes. I said that they too have consciousness and don't want to feel pain or die. "You don't really believe that, do you?" he said, incredulous and somewhat irritated. I thought there was no way to convince him at that point, but Luang Por simply asked him, in an amused way, if he thought he could get rid of all the mosquitoes by slapping them. That caught him off guard, and he admitted, "No, I guess I can't."

There was incredible energy emanating from Luang Por on those nights. We were aching from sitting so long, and Ajahn Pabhakaro and the Canadian monk who had joined us would start nodding off in their chairs, until Luang Por would rouse us with something hilariously funny. He talked about religion in the West and said, "People here follow Christianity … Santa Claus! He dresses up in his suit, the kids sit on his lap, and he says 'What would you like?'" and he did a pantomime of Santa that left us in stitches.

Earlier in one of those evenings, he talked to the visitors about death. He was aware how in Western society people cling to life and youth, and he urged us to be constantly aware of the inevitable fact of death. He said, "Imagine there was a fortune teller who'd accurately predicted the deaths of a hundred people. Then he says, 'Varapanyo is going to die in seven days.' Would you be able to sleep? I guarantee you'd ordain and meditate day and night. In fact, we're all facing the executioner. That's for certain." He said that he'd often scolded his lay followers in Thailand, because they'd been hearing about these things from the monks all their lives, yet when they were sick they'd be frightened, and if somebody died they'd be upset. He said, "If you've trained properly, there shouldn't be fear, there shouldn't be grief. When you go into the hospital for

treatment, determine 'If I get better, that's fine; if I die, that's fine.'
I guarantee you, if the doctors told me, 'Luang Por, you've got
cancer and you're going to die in a few months,' there wouldn't be
any problem at all. I'd remind the doctors, 'Watch out, it (i.e. death)
is coming to take you too, it's just a question of who goes first and
who goes later.'" He said that everyone fears cancer now, if a
person is diagnosed with cancer his family doesn't even want to tell
him about it, everyone gives up hope. He said he was once visited
by some medical researchers who were looking for cures for cancer.
He said, "These doctors aren't going to prevent death or cure
death. Only the Buddha was such a doctor. Why don't we use the
Buddha's medicine? If you are afraid of illnesses like cancer, if you
are afraid of death, you should contemplate, where do these things
really come from? They result from birth. So don't cry when
someone dies—it's just nature, and his suffering in this life is over.
If you want to cry, cry when people are born: 'Oh no, they've come
again, they're going to suffer and die again.'"

The bottom line, he said, was to give up everything for Dharma.
"What does everyone love most of all? Their own life. We can
sacrifice everything for life; if we can give our life for Dharma, there
will be no problem for us."

Some Thais in Seattle invited him for a meal. Sitting in the house
before the meal started, he talked with them about his trip and
answered a few questions. There was one of those unfortunate
young Thais present who has had too much of modern "education,"
and he had some weighty questions. Wouldn't perception of
impermanence-suffering-no self make a person want to give up
doing things and become lazy? Luang Por said that on the contrary,
one becomes more diligent, but does things without attachment,
performing only actions which are beneficial. But the man per-
sisted. If everyone practiced Dharma, nothing could be done in the
world; if everyone were to become enlightened, nobody would
make children, and humanity would become extinct. Luang Por told
him that this was like an earthworm worrying that it would run out
of dirt. On another occasion, when I told him that Westerners were
very "clever" and couldn't accept many principles of Dharma, he
said, "I once asked some learned people if they'd ever seen a

millipede. It has many legs, but how fast can it run? Can it outrun a chicken? Yet a chicken has only two legs. How come this animal with so many legs can't even keep up with a chicken?"

After the meal, Luang Por gave a Dharma talk, and someone asked about emptiness. Luang Por explained how emptiness only exists in relation to objects. There are phenomena which have the nature of being empty of real existence, thus we can talk about emptiness. It sounded exactly like the Heart Sutra, which I later translated for him.

The Kappels had arranged a "reception" for Ajahn Pabhakaro at their lodge, inviting old friends and relatives. I stayed home with Luang Por when they went, and then later in the afternoon Mr. Kappel came back to get us so that Luang Por could put in a cameo appearance. There was a large crowd and it was very noisy. I wasn't used to this kind of thing, and as I sat with Luang Por, he said, "I'm not here." I asked him where he was, and he replied, "I don't know, but I'm not here." I went into the kitchen to get some food, and Mr. Kappel was telling the staff about Ajahn Chah. "I bet this is the first time you've met a man who's never had sex" was how he described this master.

We left after a very short stay. Back in the house, I tried to sneak away to meditate, but every few minutes Luang Por would call me for one thing or another. Finally I gave up and took the tape recorder and went to sit with him. He asked about one of the people who'd been coming to see him frequently, a woman I'd known in the Hospice and the vipassana group in Santa Cruz. She had told me that she felt that Luang Por's teaching was true, but it was impossible to practice it in this society. He replied that people use similar arguments in Thailand: "I'm young so I don't have the opportunity to practice, but when I'm old I'll practice." Luang Por asked, would you say "I'm young so I don't have time to eat, when I get older I'll eat?" Again he poked me with his cane and said, if this were on fire would you say "I'm suffering, it's true, but since I live in this society I can't get away from it?" Catherine thought that Mahasi Sayadaw's approach was more suitable, i.e. doing intensive retreats from time to time in the hope that big breakthroughs would bring change. I personally was a little skeptical of that way. Many such meditators didn't practice between retreats; though Catherine tried, she felt there was very little value in it. Luang Por said, finally, that both approaches were good, if they were done thoroughly.

I mentioned that Catherine's husband liked to go rock climbing, and she felt that it was like a meditation practice for him. Luang Por asked, "When he climbs on the rocks does he see the Four Noble Truths?" I said that I didn't know, though perhaps he didn't. Then I said that sometimes I thought that when someone does a worldly activity with full attention, there can be deep concentration, for example a musician might have factors of jhana present when he plays, such as one-pointedness, rapture, etc., except that it was in an unskillful way. Luang Por just said "No ... nobody plays music and enters jhana ... only farang! ... you people don't know about jhana...."

He asked me about Zen once more, so I recited the Heart Sutra for him, doing the best I could with a spontaneous translation. When I finished he said, "No emptiness either.... No Bodhisattva...." He asked me where the sutra came from, and I said it was reputed to have been spoken by Buddha. "No Buddha." Then he said, "This is talking about deep wisdom, beyond all conventions. But it doesn't mean that we should ignore the conventions. How could we teach without them? We have to use names for things, isn't that so?"

Luang Por had arrived in Seattle around May 25, and on June 10 we flew to New York en route to Jack's center in Barre, Massachusetts. I had spent a lot of time with him answering his questions about geography, but he still couldn't put it all together. "We're in Seattle now, right? Is it a city or a state? Where are we going next? Massachusetts ... is that also America? What about Boston, is that in New York?" The Kappels were naturally sad to see Ajahn Pabhakaro leaving. Luang Por gave them a nice farewell talk and asked forgiveness for any wrong behavior. It was genuinely touching. He could be very charming or soothing if he wished.

In New York we had an unadvertised stop at my parents' house where theoretically he would get some time off before going to teach in Barre, where over 100 people were at the "Ajahn Chah Course." But some Ubon people living in New York came to see him, also he went to visit the parents of another monk, and spoke to some of my relatives and neighbors.

When he came back from visiting the monk's folks in Brooklyn, he said, "The woman can really talk. Talking and talking, no one else has to say a thing." He'd said that about some others before, including a well known Ajahn from the south of Thailand who came to Wat Bah Pong. Here I would like to digress, not for the sake of disparaging anyone, but to point out what seem to me like enormous differences between Ajahn Chah and other Theravada teachers.

The first time this Ajahn came, he was somewhat out of place, arriving with a briefcase instead of an almsbowl. I think Luang Por was away then. The Ajahn returned several months later, saying that he wanted to learn about Vinaya. As soon as he arrived he started saying, "I brought my bowl! I eat out of my bowl, I eat once a day!" He stayed for a few days, and I got to meet him when he was visiting a monk (the same monk from Brooklyn, actually) at his kuti. He seemed to be straining to appear enthusiastic about everything. One night he was at Luang Por's kuti, and I went there hoping to get a Pepsi. His conversation with Luang Por had just ended, and he was saying, "I understand now, I understand completely! Now I can go back to my wat and run it according to the Vinaya." He got up and left, and Luang Por remarked, "He must have been really inspired; he forgot to drink his Pepsi." Then he laughed and said, "He can really talk; no one else has to say anything." He left the next day. Though he had originally said that he would stay for two weeks, he left after a few days. He obviously realized he wouldn't be allowed to sit in on the Uposatha. Though he wasn't carrying money, he had a monk travelling with him who carried the loot. After the Patimokkha recitation, Luang Por spoke about this in no uncertain terms, saying what a farce it was to pretend you were keeping the Vinaya while you had another monk break it for you.

I should add that the Ajahn gave a desana to the lay people on the morning of Wun Pra, and he really charmed them—he was obviously emanating metta. He may well be highly realized, but I think his approach to Vinaya illustrated a great difference between Luang Por's way of practice and that which is followed in most other meditation temples outside of the Ajahn Mun tradition. Of course it wasn't just the one rule about money, but an indication of how one viewed the Vinaya, as a tool to use in letting go and refining the mind or merely as something to find ways around and bend to one's convenience. Generally, this Ajahn next to Luang Por seemed like a boy compared to a man, and it made me think that Luang Por's way of practice has a great dignity to it that might not be found elsewhere, among those who seek shortcuts or simply don't understand how the Buddha intended monastic life to be used.

Of course, I am partial to Ajahn Chah. I realize a good case could be made for other approaches to Vinaya—e.g. in 1987 I had a discussion with a veteran German monk who simply said, "The rules are for idiots. They're just common sense; if you can use common sense, you don't need to worry about rules." Upon considering this, I thought that if someone is free of the grosser forms of mental turbulence and is able to apply himself one-pointedly to meditation practice, worrying about details of conduct might well be superfluous. It's a big subject.

I've also come to feel that there may be a big difference in his view of Path-Fruit-Nirvana from some Theravada masters who have become popular. It may be just a matter of terminology and teaching styles—I am in no position to say for certain. Most of his disciples know that he didn't talk a whole lot about Nirvana and the levels of enlightenment from Sotapanna to Arhat. His simile of himself as a tree in reply to the question "Are you an Arhat?" reminded me of the Diamond Sutra, in which Buddha asks, "What do you think, Subhuti, does an Arhat have the thought, 'I have attained the stage of Arhat'?" and the answer is "No, World Honored One. Wherefore? Because if he had the thought, 'I have attained something,' this would be self-grasping, and not the Arhat stage. It is precisely because he has no such thoughts that he is called 'Arhat'." When I see how many practicers become crazed by the idea of attaining the stages which many teachers put forth, I wonder if it is just a difference in means or a real difference in view. I will just add one more note, that according to some Mahayana texts, the attainments of the "lesser vehicle" are incomplete because there is still a subtle sense of self involved, i.e. there is someone who escapes from suffering and attains liberation. Again, there's no telling what Luang Por might have said if one had asked the right questions; but

143

his life of selfless service to others leaves little question but that he embodied the ideal of a Bodhisattva, and he showed time and again that he wasn't attached to the labels and concepts which indicate limited understanding.

When we arrived in Barre the retreat had already begun. The staff took us on a tour of the place and showed us to our rooms. I was exhausted from trying to keep up with Luang Por, and when the manager told me my room was next to Luang Por's, he seemed a little surprised when I said, "Oh no! I was hoping I'd be on the other side of the building from him."

For the remaining eight days of the retreat he gave group interviews in the afternoon and a few evening talks. In the morning he would talk with the staff before the meal, and occasionally people would come to his room at night. Much of it is on tape in Barre.

For his morning sessions with the staff, he quickly established the theme of facing the executioner. When people came in he would ask, "Did you do your work today?" He told them they should think about death at least three times in a day, once in the morning, afternoon, and evening. "Don't be like Po (that's what he'd started calling me; it's the Thai corruption of the Pali "bodhi", i.e. enlightenment, and commonly used as a name)" he'd say. "He just walks around, he looks at the trees and the birds, he eats his lunch, he never thinks that he's going to die someday." I became the straight man for him, and would sometimes prompt him with questions. The idea of death is usually remote, I once told him. If I felt some danger, it might be more real. "Don't you see the danger?" he said. "Every breath." I said that I usually felt that for me, death was far in the future, I was destined to live a long time, 100 years or more. "That's the wisdom of Devadatta," he replied.

In the group interviews he generally gave direct and simple answers to complicated questions. He told people to put the books away, to rely on themselves, to have determination and perseverance. One person asked, "When I try to sit and follow my breathing, my mind starts wandering, then I get pain in my legs which makes me think even more ... How would you suggest I deal with it?" Luang Por said, "Deal with it just like that." People laughed, but he said to really determine the mind to see it through, and to realize how these conditions of mind and body are impermanent and empty.

People would continually talk about the difficulties they faced as lay practicers. He said that it was difficult to practice as a house-holder; it's like trying to meditate in prison. You sit down and begin, and the prison officer comes and shouts, "Get up! March over there!" He also compared it to sitting on an ant hill: the ants are biting, the person becomes uncomfortable but refuses to get up and move somewhere else. Or you come to the Ajahn holding some-thing burning hot in your hand, and you complain, "Ajahn, this is hot!" The Ajahn says, "So put it down," and you say, "I can't put it down ... but I don't want it to be hot!" So what can the Ajahn do for you? He again emphasized getting at the root causes of things. You go for a walk and you trip over a stump, so you get a hatchet and cut it. But it grows back and you trip over it again, so you cut it again. But it keeps on growing back. You'd better get a tractor and plow it up. I said, "I don't know where I'll get a tractor from," and he answered something like "you have to find out where they come from." In summary, he said it's like asking yourself, should I go today, should I? ... maybe I'll go tomorrow ... Then the next day, should I go, should I or shouldn't I? and you keep on doing this day after day until you die, and you never go anywhere. You've got to think, Go! and that's it.

Someone asked about the state of the world, if we could help the world or if there was hope for the world. He replied, "You're asking about the world. Do you know what the world is? It's just the senses and their objects, and the ignorance that grasps at them. The Pali word for 'world' is *loko,* which means darkness; the opposite of it, *aloko,* means light. Through meditation we can realize the light which shines above the world's darkness."

In Seattle someone had asked him to describe how he prepared his mind for meditation, and he said, "I just keep it where it always is." In Barre someone asked him to talk about enlightenment; could he describe his own enlightenment? With everyone eagerly await-ing the answer to this one, Luang Por said, "Enlightenment is not difficult (to understand). Just take a banana and put it in your mouth—then you will know what it tastes like." This brought the house down. I was translating, so I added that he obviously meant that you can, and must, know it for yourself, but it reminded me of the Zen stories of people becoming enlightened upon seeing flowers in bloom, etc., so maybe they would want to try it with a banana sometime.

One afternoon when the session was over, I was unplugging my tape recorder and I touched the metal prong of the plug while it was still connected. I got a shock and dropped it immediately. Luang Por noticed, and he said, "Oh! How come you could let go of that so easily? Who told you to?" It was a good illustration of what he was trying to teach.

Finally he told people they were always welcome to come to his wat and stay for a while. Wat Bah Pong is like a factory, he said. After the product is finished it can be sent out into the world. But it's easier to train people if they're far from their home. "Po ran away," he said. "If I were younger, I'd drag him back by his ear."

I had called one ex-monk, Jim, who had spent most of his monastic years with other teachers but regarded Luang Por highly, to tell him that Luang Por would be in Barre, and he came and stayed for a few days. He had been a Dhammayut monk for several frustrating years, and after a few visits to Wat Bah Pong decided he'd like to stay there, but Sangha politics prevented that. I saw him occasionally, and though he didn't do much practice as a layman, I figured he'd like to see Luang Por. He arrived as we were taking a walk. He came up to Luang Por, knelt down, and "wai'ed." He was fat (though not as fat as I'd seen him the year before), not quite the image of a Dharma practicer, and Luang Por immediately started abusing him. Jim admitted that he'd gotten far from the Dharma, and Luang Por pointed to rne and said, "Why can't you be like him? He disrobed but he practices diligently." I thought that was pretty cute, considering how he usually held me up as the model of what not to do. But Jim humbly accepted the criticism. During his stay Luang Por was able to reach him with his stern humor and gentle advice, and he left with some inspiration that he hadn't felt in a long time, thanking me for inviting him and vowing to practice.

Several people there said Ajahn Chah was very much like Zen teachers they had known. He often came up with the same similes that past and present masters have used, and which I'm sure he'd never read or heard. There were some people at the center who'd been with the Korean Zen master, Seung Sahn, and had left him to find greener pastures among the Theravadins, but now Ajahn Chah was teaching just as he had. "You thought you'd get away from it, but you can't," Luang Por laughed. When we were driving around downtown Seattle one day, Luang Por said that the people in the city were like a dog who sees his reflection in a window and gets all excited, thinking it's another dog. It reminded me of a Huang Po simile, of a mad dog barking at the wind in the grass, i.e. perceiving something where nothing is really happening; also the simile of the dog who wants to drink from a pond, but when he approaches it sees his reflection and runs away from the "dog in the water."

All in all, I think he had a favorable impression of Western practicers. He could see how crazy the society was and how deep people's confusion and suffering went, but I think he appreciated their sincerity in seeking a way out, and he saw a large group of people working hard at the retreat. He said he was sorry he hadn't come when he was younger and would have been able to do more. And once he made the mysterious pronouncement that he would come back in 30 years and establish a monastery.

At the end of the retreat we all did a ceremony of asking forgiveness. He gave some final advice, and Jack gave a short talk in which he put Luang Por's visit in the perspective of being part of the beginning of the transmission of the Buddhadharma to the West, and reminded us how fortunate we were to be taking part in it.

Zen Master Seung Sahn came for a visit. They had two brief chats, and though it was low-key, there was a very nice feeling about their meeting. Luang Por enjoyed Seung Sahn's Zen stories, told him a little about life in his wat, and listened to what Seung Sahn had to say about his experience in the West. I wasn't really sure how Luang Por felt about him, since he often acted skeptical about other teachers, but when they parted he said with sincerity, "May you be a great Bodhi tree to give shelter to many people here." Apparently Seung Sahn was favorably impressed with Luang Por, as he later wrote the introduction to *Still Forest Pool*.

One of the stories Seung Sahn told was about the Zen monk who sneaks into a lecture hall where some great scholar is talking about One Mind. "All things come from the one mind," the scholar teaches, at which the Zen monk comes forth and challenges him.

"You say all things come from the one mind. OK. So now tell me, where does the one mind come from?" When the preacher was unable to answer, the monk beat him. Luang Por laughed and said, "He deserved a beating, all right." Afterwards he repeated this several times, laughing and saying what a good story that was: "He couldn't answer where the one mind comes from, so he really deserved a beating."

Luang Por and I had a lot of fun together on that trip. He would say things like, "Staying here with Varapanyo is OK, maybe I won't go back to Thailand," or "I shouldn't enjoy being with such a person, but I do." Someone at Barre said that we were like a couple of drinking partners sitting at the bar, getting high and making each other laugh. Of course it's preposterous to suggest any kind of equality, but since disrobing I hadn't had such an experience of being with someone who saw things as I did; it felt very natural and very refreshing.

When the retreat ended he went to visit Anicca Farm, a piece of land where several practicers were living. I stayed at the center and caught up on sleep. He came back two days later, and it was time to see him off at the airport. He was on his way to England, where the Sangha was about to move to its own forest sanctuary at Chithurst. He had me take a copy of the retreat schedule for him and translate it into Thai. He said he was going to do something like that when he got back to Wat Bah Pong, "except we'll have to change '6 PM—Tea' to '6 PM—Borapet'. (Borapet is an extremely bitter medicinal vine. It provided the only evening beverage at Wat Bah Pong in the early years.)

So Luang Por disappeared through the passenger gate at Logan Airport and I took the shuttle flight to New York. The following week I went back to California. I felt highly inspired and did a retreat in my cabin there. I had a dozen tapes from the trip and listened to them over and over again, until I knew them all word for word.

In February of 1980 I was also doing a retreat at the cabin when I received a copy of *Bodhinyana,* a book of translations of Luang Por's teachings, in the mail. It was very timely, and made me want to see Luang Por again. But I had to wait until the fall of the following year, when I finally managed to get money together for a trip to Thailand.

IX

"Thus it is said, 'Behold the nature of the Guru, that naked awareness of Shunyata.'"

I was planning the trip for almost a year. In December 1980 I got a job working with Indo-Chinese refugees, which provided the money and also gave me practice in speaking Thai and Lao again. Somehow I imagined that I'd just be visiting; I planned to go to other Buddhist countries as well, especially Japan, since I'd been practicing Zen for a while. But once when I was discussing it with a friend, he said "I guess you're going there for a retreat." I explained that Wat Bah Pong wasn't exactly a retreat center, but then I realized I wasn't going to be a tourist, either; living in the wat I would naturally be practicing with the monks. Keeping in mind the old adage "If the government catches you, they'll flog you to death; if the Buddhists catch you, they'll starve you to death," I prepared for a return to austere living.

Jack had been at Wat Bah Pong in early 1981, and I spoke to him before leaving in November. From what he said, it sounded like business as usual there. I expected that I would go stay with Luang Por and see what developed. I didn't know about his latest illness and the surgery it had led to.

As Jack had predicted, it felt very nice to be back in Thailand, to walk around Bangkok in the deafening noise and suffocating smog, to eat noodles and chat with people. I spent a few days recovering from my 30 hour plane trip, visiting a few old friends and planning to go to Ubon soon. Then when I went to Wat Boworn one day, the farang monks there told me about Luang Por: he'd just had surgery for water on the brain and was in Bangkok, at Samrong Hospital. Ajahn Pabhakaro was looking after him, and access was restricted.

So I took a very long bus ride to Samrong, only to be told that Luang Por had left the day before. He was staying somewhere off Sukhumvit Road, but they didn't know the address. Well that's the way it is, I thought, and headed for the door to take the bus back to Banglampoo. Then I thought I should probably use the toilet before getting on the bus for another one and a half or two hours. As I walked to the bathroom, I saw a familiar face attached to a body sitting in the outpatient area. I realized it was someone from Ubon—it was Por Juang of Ban Gaw village, near Wat Bah Pong. He recognized me. I asked him what he was doing there, and he told me that he was in Bangkok with Luang Por. He'd come to get his teeth fixed at the hospital, and someone was going to take him back to the place where Luang Por was staying, so why didn't I wait and go with him?

In the old days I used to think, "What did you do in Thailand?" "I waited." When someone says, "sit down and wait just a little bit," or "they'll be here in an hour at most" you can prepare to be waiting a long, long time. Por Juang said that someone was coming soon. I figured that at any rate, getting a ride in "someone's" car would beat taking the bus. So we sat and waited, and waited. Finally the doctor's son came to take us—on the bus. About 45 minutes later we got off at Soi 81 and started walking down the soi, but couldn't find the address. Por Juang had been there just a few hours before, but Bangkok was so strange to him that he might as well have been on Mars (actually, he usually did act like he was on Mars), and the doctor's son had never been there before. I suggested asking people on the street where the house was—from the way those two were floundering around I figured that such an idea would never occur to them—but nobody recognized the address. We walked up and down the soi, wading through those black puddles which are so unique to Bangkok, until we saw a mailman, who told us there was no such address on that soi. I was getting tired and a little irritated—I'd been through similar routines many times in the past in Thailand,

and now here I was, just back for a few days and it was happening again. I realized that maybe I wouldn't be able to find Luang Por. It was disappointing, but I considered that I had come to be in the forest, not the city, so how bad could it be if I just went to Ubon in a couple of days? Still, I held on to the hope of seeing Luang Por, though it seemed to be slipping away fast, and I asked Por Juang, "You were just here this morning, can't you remember the house?" He apologized, "Kanoy, it all looks the same to me." Then he started saying, "Luang Por's staying at the house of 'Je Salee'; he's staying with 'Je Salee,'" for anyone who happened to be listening. We were heading back towards Sukhumvit Road, and the bus stop, when he recognized a water tower. We walked up to a driveway, and saw Luang Por standing with Ajahn Pabhakaro at the other end. It was a very long driveway, but I thought I could feel Luang Por's eyes on me, and imagined him smirking.

We walked down the driveway to him. He was putting on his robe to take a walk, and the first thing he said was, "Did Grandpa die?" I had once told him that I would someday inherit some money from my grandfather. He apparently remembered. After I disrobed, one of the monks wrote that "Luang Por said that Varapanyo must be waiting for that relative of his to die so he can come to Thailand." I told him that Grandpa was alive and well; I had gotten a job and earned some money for the plane fare.

He told me about his operation as we strolled up and down the driveway. He said that he was very weak and still had dizzy spells. "Being old is no fun, Varapanyo," he said, holding his head.

It was about five weeks since the operation. Though he was in a weakened physical condition, his mind was the same as ever. He didn't give Dharma talks to the lay people—"Je Salee" was Mrs. Kesaree, who had built a large kuti on her property, and she and her friends were ardent Dharma students—but he would still hang out and chat with people. His sense of humor hadn't lost anything. Monks and lay people came in a continuous flow. In the morning he still took his meal with whichever monks were there, though he didn't go pindapat. The doctors had said that he would need six months of rest. I doubt that anyone could have imagined at that point how his condition was to deteriorate in the near future. I went to see him almost every day, and he would keep me there until late

151

at night, massaging him while he insulted me, until I would have to beg leave of him to catch one of the last buses (I must add in all fairness that he had invited me to stay there—to sleep on the lawn without a mosquito net). But still I was restless to get out of the city and go to Ubon. A few months later, when it was too late, I realized what a precious opportunity that had been, both in that I could spend long hours with him, and that it would be the last time he was really himself and wasn't being closely guarded. It made me look back on his trip to America as well. At the time I didn't consider that it might be a once in a lifetime occurrence, and I know I didn't appreciate it as much as I should have, always trying to sneak away from him to meditate, spending too much of the precious time scheming about my future or wishing I were somewhere else.

At times it was obvious that he tired very quickly. He would get bleary-eyed while he was sitting with guests, and it was a great effort for him to pay attention and talk with them. But people were coming from all over—disciples from Ubon, Ayuthaya, and other places, often in big groups, and Bangkok people who'd just heard of him and were curious—and everyone wanted to get their turn, nobody wanted to be denied a piece of the action. I think it was probably a new and difficult situation for the monks and lay people who were supposed to be looking after Luang Por. They knew he had to have rest but they didn't feel good about turning people away.

When Luang Por was in the U.S. he said many times that I was not really a layman, though not a monk either. Over the years I realized that much of lay life was alien to me and would probably remain that way always, and that my training combined with my predispositions made me think pretty much like a monk. Now that I was in Thailand again, many people spoke to me as if I were a monk, i.e. they used the honorific forms of speech (or in the case of monks, would use the forms for speaking to an equal), and I encountered this not only with people I had known, but with some I had just met. My hair was quite short, but I thought it was a little strange since there are no lay priests in Thai Buddhism, and it's pretty hard to mistake blue jeans and a sport shirt for a yellow robe. Ajahn Pabhakaro claimed that the day I went to the hospital, they called Kesaree's house saying, "There's a farang monk who's come to see Luang Por Chah—except he's not a monk!" This was to continue for years in Bangkok and Ubon—people calling me Ajahn, some even giving me money, a dentist who insisted on treating me for free. It was one of the things that made me come to appreciate Thailand much more than I had as a monk, when I usually felt like a prisoner sweating out my karma in a tropical Siberia, and made me feel like I was living off my merits (it was nice to think that I had some merits to live off of).

It was also extraordinary to see the generosity of donors who support the monks in Thailand, and to contemplate the role of religion and the Sangha in the society. As a monk one may come to take it all for granted, but having been away I was now seeing it with new eyes. In Western countries nothing remotely like it exists, but even in other Buddhist countries the Dharma and Sangha don't play such an important part in people's lives. Even the ordinary monks, whom I had never held in great esteem, seemed to fulfill a useful purpose, providing a way for people to practice generosity and contributing somewhat to the moral force which I suspect sustains the country.

Being a monk, or living with monks, one sees the best side of people. It may not be their only side, but nevertheless it's genuine. The yellow robe is often spoken of as the "banner of the Arhats" and it is a symbol that people respect and that can turn their minds towards virtue, and it doesn't necessarily depend on the character of the person wearing the robe. There are abuses, of course, but in Thailand it still works pretty well for the most part. In the poorer Northeast I found the devotion of the people especially inspiring. Many of them exist at or near subsistence level, but they always give a portion of what they have. As a visiting lay practicer, it felt like a great privilege to eat almsfood that was given in faith; it occasionally even spurred me to make some effort in practice.

So I spent a week riding the #2 bus back and forth across town, from Wat Boworn in Banglampoo to Kesaree's in Pra Kanong, and hanging out with Luang Por. One afternoon I accompanied him on his daily walk down the driveway. There was a nursery or some such thing next to the driveway, and the babies were all crying. He pointed up to where the sound was coming from and asked if that's what I wanted. I said no, I didn't think so, but I added, "I figure if the mind is in the right place, then there's no problem anywhere; one could go to hell and it wouldn't be hot." All Luang Por said to me was, "You just talk."

In his moments of fatigue he came out with short, penetrating statements like that, as if he were getting the same amount of wisdom, and humor, into fewer words. There were several American Vipassana students in town, some ordained and staying at Wat Boworn, and they hoped to be able to see Luang Por. When I tried to mention it to him, he cut me off with, "Farang? Why do you want to bring farang here?" but Ajahn Pabhakaro interpreted this to mean that it would be OK, I didn't really need to ask. They came in two groups, one at meal time and the other in the afternoon. He sat outside on the lawn when he received the second group, and when one of the Thai people suggested that he might wish to rest, he said he wanted to talk with his Dharma friends. He looked very tired, but he answered a few questions. One newly ordained novice asked what his advice for new people was. "The same as for old people." And what was that? "Keep at it." Someone else said, I can observe desire and aversion in my mind, but it's hard to observe delusion. "You're riding on a horse and asking 'where's the horse?'," was Luang Por's answer, though at first I had thought that he said, "You're shovelling dogshit and asking 'where's the dog?'" which may be just as good. An American nun said she had a problem with desire for attainment, to which he answered, "drop it." I know I should drop it, she said, but I keep holding on to it. "So drop it."

(As I'm retyping, I feel that I may be making Ajahn Chah appear pretty cantankerous, at times even sadistic. It's hard for me to convey in words the warmth and vitality that were usually present in him [excepting those times when he chose to turn them off]. I should also point out that he once described his approach to teaching as corrective: he sees people walking down a road, and if he notices a ditch on the left that they don't see, he'll shout, "go right." When he knows there's danger or obstruction to the right, he shouts, "go left." His aim was not to merely be contrary, but to help.)

Though he was alive, he wasn't all that well, and a phrase would occasionally go through my head: "Who killed Luang Por?" His case, and those of some teachers who'd gone to the West, made me think that having a lot of western disciples was a heavy burden. We obviously had a lot of suffering, and therefore heavy karma, in order to have sought him out, and we were much more extreme in our behavior and probably our mind-states than Asian disciples. But it was also obvious that Luang Por really liked teaching people who were sincerely interested. In the past, no matter how tired he was, he'd almost always come alive if he had a receptive (or, better yet, inquisitive) audience. Maybe that took a lot of energy and wore him down in the long run, but transmitting the Dharma to people who wanted to be liberated was his purpose in being alive in the first place.

After a week with Luang Por I finally decided to go to Ubon. The days of my visa were passing. As a layman I'd gotten into the habit of going to retreats, seven or ten days of relative calm and sanity which I learned to prize, and I unfortunately brought that mentality with me on my trip. It was to be many months before I could let go of it a little. I stopped to visit a friend who was working at a refugee camp in Surin, and then took the milkrun train, which let me off at Bung Wai village in the afternoon. The station master and I recognized each other, and he offered to drive me to the wat on his motorcycle.

It was late afternoon when I entered the wat, and the insects were beginning their incredible symphony. I went into the sala and in the fading light saw several of my old cronies. They had come for a meeting of the Sangha at the request of Ajahn Jagaro, the Australian monk who was then abbot at Wat Bung Wai, to discuss the new visa regulations for foreign monks. It was the day after Wun Pra and they were just hanging out after the weekly sauna. Needless to say, it was good to see all those venerable faces. We chatted for a little while, someone got me set up in the guest room above the kitchen, and in the evening I went and visited with Ajahn Jagaro.

Wat Bung Wai had grown—there were more and sturdier kutis, a new kitchen and abbot's kuti, etc.—but the strongest impression was how it had matured as a place of training and practice. After several years' experience, the Western monks were able to run a monastery very smoothly. It seemed that everything was done harmoniously and well. I had feared that it would be a "cold turkey" to be living like that again, but actually I felt quite at home. Living without distractions, practicing in the company of those who were leading a pure life, was refreshing and uplifting. There was a very positive feeling among the monks, and visitors like myself were treated with great kindness. At that time I knew about half the monks from the "old days," but I found that after a short time I was relating to the newer monks as old friends. Perhaps my notoriety as Varapanyo had something to do with it. I suppose they had all heard Luang Por tell stories about me, and I had also left some translation work behind. The lay people treated me with so much respect that it was at times embarrassing, and I thought it probably looked a little strange to the younger monks.

Sitting in a kuti in the forest once again, I felt very pleased with myself that I'd stepped out of the routines I'd gotten into as a layman and was now able to take a clear look at things—though at times it was horrifying to see how I'd spent some of my time. Practicing in the sala with the monks was very inspiring, meeting early in the morning to chant and meditate without ulterior motives. Simple acts like sweeping the floor of the sala before dawn, in silence, seemed to be full of grace and beauty. Of course it wasn't happening in some celestial place: it was difficult to be getting up at 3 AM again, there were mosquitoes just as there had always been, the concrete floor hadn't gotten any softer, and some mornings it was a struggle just to sit through it until the bell rang, at which time I could take a break although the monks had to go out for pindapat. Many mornings I would sit there in the back row where the laymen sit and ask myself, "How do they do it?!" Sometimes I would wonder how I did it once upon a time. I began to think that when a person disrobed after a few years of monkhood, he should be given a certificate of honor, rather than being called a bum and kicked out in disgrace.

Then I came down with flu, which took much of my inspiration away and reminded me of what it was often like there. "I came here to meditate and have a good time, not to see suffering," I told one monk.

I was there for the Christmas celebration, which came on Wun Pra that year. In the morning Ajahn Jagaro gave a very good talk to the lay people about the common purpose of religions. I was pleased to see how he and the others had developed over the years. He in particular had plodded along, plagued by doubt, for many years, but had clearly gotten through it and was now quite capable of teaching others, and finding much joy in it as well. Here was Luang Por Chah's legacy, and it was of such a nature that, unlike worldly things, the more it was shared with others, the more it would continue to increase. Just walking through the forest I often felt that Luang Por's mind was there, or that it had all manifested out of his mind (with considerable help from Ajahn Sumedho insofar as the Westerners are concerned). Especially now, when Ajahn Chah is pretty much a vegetable, I feel like I see a lot more of him in the forest of one of his monasteries than I do when I go to pay respects to his body at Wat Bah Pong.

One day I walked over to Wat Bah Pong. The monks at Bung Wai had told me that I wouldn't recognize much of it—land had been bought up all around the wat, another gate built in front, and the bote was completed. All of this was striking, but when I walked around in the forest and went to Luang Por's old kuti, it was like being transported back in time. The ghosts of various emotions and memories all seemed to appear at once, and it was overwhelming. I've visited Wat Bah Pong several times since then, and the same thing always happens. I may have worked through lifetimes' worth of karma in my few years at Wat Bah Pong, but the ghosts still hang out there, and we still recognize each other. In the case of Luang Por's kuti, though, I'm sure there's more to it than just my own experiences. Even now it calms the mind to go there, prostrate to his empty seat, sweep the floor and remove a few cobwebs.

A couple of monks recognized me and called me over to chat. They both seemed content as monks and dedicated to practice, even without Luang Por around to goad and inspire. There was a lot of noise going around because a few senior monks had disrobed, including Ajahn Sinuan—I had brought some small gifts for him only to find out that he was now tending buffaloes—but it was reassuring to see that there were still a lot of monks who were just quietly going about their business.

I wanted to visit some of the branch monasteries of Wat Bah Pong and some of the Ajahns I'd known, so a few days after Christmas I accompanied a new monk who was going to stay at Beung Kow Luang to train with Ajahn Jun. The trip there was a Thai "classic." We rushed into town to make an 11 AM truck, except it was leaving at 12, so we waited in the store of a lay supporter. When the truck did leave, it drove around town picking up passengers and goods for transport, and after an hour we were still in Ubon, though at least on the side of town closer to Amper Keuang Ny, which is where we wanted to go. The driver stopped at yet one more shop, turned off the engine, and went to eat lunch. I was starting to fume, sitting there in the oven-like cab of the truck. I went and got bags of Pepsi with ice in them, offered one to the monk, drank mine standing outside the truck, then stomped up and down the street until it was time to leave again. This kind of thing had happened many times in the past. When it happens now, I get the feeling that I've never left, this is what life is, this is what I must always endure until the end of time, and I get impatient and depressed. So I fumed all the way to Beung Kow Luang—at least we got a ride right to the monastery—as the driver stopped on almost every corner to pick up passengers and discuss business, family, fermented fish and weather with people along the way.

We walked into the monastery, and a novice took us to sit in the bote while he went to get Ajahn Jun. Ajahn Jun recognized me, though he wasn't sure of my name. The monk gave him a letter from Ajahn Jagaro. He read it out loud—basically just an introduction and a request to train this fellow appropriately—and then he remarked to the Thai monks and novices who had gathered, "These farang write Thai better than you guys" (which is often true, many rural people having only gone to school four years so that they can barely read the chanting books and write their names).

Ajahn Jun asked me about lay life, if I still meditated, did any teaching, etc. I told him I still practiced, sometimes led meditations in the group I'd been involved in, occasionally gave a Dharma talk. He said, that's good, you learned how to practice here and now you can continue in the world and share what you've learned with others. But he was sure to tell Nimmalo, the monk who'd come with me, "You don't have to disrobe. Varapanyo will take care of things

out there, and you stay here." In the fashion of Luang Por, he was
to embellish things a little, and would tell the monks and lay people,
"We have a visitor, Ajahn Varapanyo, he's a Vipassana Ajahn, he
trained at Wat Bah Pong and now he's an Ajahn, spreading
Buddhism in America. ... "

Beung Kow Luang felt even nicer than Bung Wai—it's bigger
and quieter—and as I moved on to visit the branch monasteries,
each place seemed better than the last. But I had unfortunately
arrived in time for New Year's Eve. In the past we used to sit up until
midnight at Wat Bah Pong for New Year's, the lay people would
come and we did some chanting to bring in the new year on an
auspicious note. A lot of people had gathered at Beung Kow Luang
for the occasion. In the afternoon Ajahn Jun started playing taped
Dharma talks over his loudspeakers. We gathered for chanting,
then he played some more tapes, then he began one of his
talkathons. I must say that I enjoy his Dharma more than that of any
other Thai disciples of Ajahn Chah, but as the night wore on my
knees got mighty sore, and it all began to seem rather pointless.
Midnight came, the monks did some chanting, he talked some
more, then about 1 AM he took out a Vinaya text and started
reading from that, explaining it in his most polite central Thai
instead of the country Lao that he'd been talking in, as if he just
knew that everyone was keenly interested. We got out of the sala
around 1:30-2:00. The next morning after the meal he was at it
again. So I decided not to stay too long, and was soon on my way
to Wat Tam Saeng Pet (a few months later Nimmalo also left for
Tam Saeng Pet, because his knees started to give out due to sitting
through long desanas).

After several hours of travelling I was in Amnat Jaroen, where
I had to get on a truck for a ten km ride and then walk another three
km to the wat. I was carrying a heavy pack but there was no other
way save hiring a truck at exorbitant rates to take me right to the
wat. I was asking where to board a truck when a teenage boy with
a shaved head approached me. "You're going to Wat Tam Saeng
Pet, aren't you? Just wait a moment, I'm getting a car to take me,"
he said. It sounded good; but this was Thailand. It turned out that
his sister lived nearby and she had a car. Where does she live? I
asked suspiciously. Right over there, he said. We started walking.

It was a little further than "right over there" and my pack was heavy. He left me by the roadside to wait while he ran down a path towards a rice mill. I waited for a while, and watched pickup trucks go by. Bad manners and common sense were by now telling me to get on one of them, but I waited. Finally he came back. No car. So we walked back up the road a way and waited for a pickup truck. He insisted on getting off before the turnoff to Tam Saeng Pet in order to take a "shortcut." We walked for a very long time. I felt like strangling him, but instead merely insisted on stopping to catch my breath once. He offered to carry my pack part of the way. "Hey, this is really heavy," he said as he struggled with it.

Though it always happens that way, I was asking myself, as I usually do, "Why does it always have to happen this way?" and I entertained briefly the notion that Thais may be mentally deficient as a race and pondered possible causes. Finally we were at the top of the hill, the big open air sala was up ahead. As I went up the steps, Ajahn Vitoon came in from the other side. He gave me a very nice welcome, just as Ajahn Jun had and others would later on. An English monk had arrived from Bung Wai a few days before and had told him that I was coming, and I suspect that he had gone over all the old Varapanyo stories in his mind. He invited me to stay as long as I wished. I stayed in Ajahn Sumedho's old cave and practiced on my own, no questions asked, only coming out for the morning meal and an afternoon bath. The "Milarepa Cave" as it was called was one of the more secluded places in the wat, which is unfortunately one of the favorite tourist and picnic spots in Ubon Province, and I stayed for two weeks.

Wat Tam Saeng Pet is very large, several hundred acres, and it has been divided into two monasteries, though not because of its size. It is one of the sadder stories in the history of Ajahn Chah and Wat Bah Pong. Luang Por and others had great hopes for it, and on this trip I often thought of the great monasteries in ancient China where 1000 or more monks would live, and I figured they were probably in locations like this. So now, may I introduce the villain of the piece, Ajahn Som. The way I heard it, he was there first, and then invited Luang Por to send monks and make it a branch monastery. There were a couple of wealthy supporters to build things and supply food, but nobody could live with Ajahn Som, who apparently was telling his monks that meditation was a waste of time, it was better just to work all day. Still, farang monks were usually able to live there because he would let them meditate as they wished, so some may still be fond of him. When my sister visited me we went there and he was a very gracious host. I thus thought well of him for a long time, but when I started going there to practice as a layman there was no getting around the fact that he'd ruined what could have been a great thing for many people. He was also pretty cantankerous when I went to pay my respects to him, and I did my best to avoid him after that.

Luang Por had often talked about moving his abbots around, and he would especially have liked to move Ajahn Som, but the latter said that he would disrobe and re-ordain Dhammayut if Luang Por did that. The other senior monks weren't as bad—they would just grin sheepishly and look at the floor whenever Luang Por mentioned it. They usually were settled in monasteries near their home villages, and Luang Por said they were attached to their situation, and he thought it might be better for everyone to move them around. Yet none of them took the hint. I'm sure that if Luang Por would have asked any of the farang abbots, in Thailand or in England, to pick up and move, there wouldn't have been the slightest hesitation, so it makes me wonder what the extent of people's commitment to him really was.

One of the special attractions of Tam Saeng Pet was that it's three km from the nearest village, so the noise of village festivals and movie shows doesn't reach the monastery at night. Unfortunately such noise is pretty common almost everywhere now, because the electric lines have reached most of the villages, and the villages have spread out to get closer to the wats. I remember very little of it from my first years in Thailand, but now it's spread like the plague.

When I was leaving, Ajahn Vitoon invited me to come back whenever I was in the neighborhood, and it turned out that I visited there many times in the years to come. But by now the kutis in the best caves are all falling apart, those remaining have been poisoned with DDT, and the place is constantly swarming with local tourists who behave much worse than the village dogs that come to scavenge for food. Illegal loggers trespass with chain saws, as they do in forests all over the country, gunshots are heard occasionally as hunters chase small game; sometimes they try to smoke the animals out of the woods, then flee and leave the forest to burn when the monks apprehend them. Ajahn Som has built some gaudy Buddhas and, against Sangha rules, installed donation boxes, so he is encouraging the people who come with their radios and bottles of whiskey. Ajahn Vitoon complains about it but does little to stop it. I'm getting depressed as I type this, it reminds me how hard it's getting to find a quiet place in Thailand, and I fear it's a prime example of how population growth and modernization combine to erode the quality of life.

My next stop was a small monastery on the road back to Ubon, where Luang Por Laht was staying. He's an old man who ordained around age 60, a serious practicer and one of Ajahn Chah's favorites. I remembered that he had been troubled by a skin disease and severe back pain, and I asked Ajahn Vitoon if he was still alive. Ajahn Vitoon had gone out to a meal in town while I was at Tam Saeng Pet, and he met Por Laht there and told him I'd asked about him. "Huoi!" he said, "everyone asks the same thing: 'Is Por Laht still alive? Por Laht hasn't died yet?' I was asking myself, 'Is Varapanyo still alive?'"

I walked into the wat in early afternoon. There was a small sala but no monks in sight. I went around to the back of the sala and saw Por Laht taking a nap under a tree. He heard me coming and woke up, and immediately got up to put out a mat and get me some water.

I think he said he was 74 then, and he was still pretty lively. "I'm finished with the world, Varapanyo. 'It' is stuck to my testicles," he said, using a local idiom for the state of dispassion and non-arousal. "I haven't handled money in 10 years, 15 years. I don't even know what the new bills look like." He was living alone, doing his practice, morning and evening chanting, all night sittings on Wun Pra. He suggested I stay there with him. I asked if he had requested monks from Luang Por. He said he'd gone to Wat Bah Pong to ask Luang Por to give him a monk and a novice, but "he got angry and told me to come back here and die." Actually, many of the branch monasteries are now "understaffed," and Por Laht's monastery was very small, so I think Luang Por knew that while it might be difficult, Por Laht could probably hold the fort by himself and use the difficulty and solitude to further his practice.

I stayed two nights. We had several nice talks. He asked me what I was up to. "That's good," he said about my lay life. "You study different things, you can come and teach me Path-Fruit-Nirvana." He remembered several of the foreign monks he'd lived with. "Sumedho's gone to England, Jack's in America, Varapanyo travels all over, Khemadhammo's a hermit somewhere ... after this life we'll all meet up in Nirvana." He was very solicitous of my comfort while I was there. He sent for one of the villagers to take me to his house and give me dinner because he was worried I'd be hungry. In the afternoon he refused to let me haul water, afraid I'd get tired.

It was obvious that he had no illusions about the world anymore, and I really felt that he'd surrendered to the Dharma. When I saw Luang Por the following month, I said, "Por Laht's surrendered." Luang Por said, "He's too feeble to go anywhere anymore, so he's surrendered."

From there I went back to Bung Wai. It almost felt like going home. Things were in transition then. Ajahn Jagaro was preparing to go to Australia. Ajahn Pasanno was to be the new abbot, but he was away part of the time since his parents were in Bangkok. So there were a few people taking turns as senior monk, but everything continued to run smoothly.

One morning, well before the bell, I woke up with cramps in my stomach. I reached for my kettle to pour some water, only to get a cup full of ants. It seemed like a classic forest wat episode. After morning chanting I said to one of the monks, "I want to see the manager." "He's on vacation," was the answer. I told him what had happened. "That's what it's all about," he said.

When my visa was up I planned to go to Sri Lanka, but I went to Bangkok early with the hope of spending time with Luang Por. It was not to be. I knew that he had moved outside of town to Samut Sakorn, about 50 km to the south, to stay in a kuti some doctor had built near the ocean. This was a better place for him to be, but his physical condition had gone down drastically, and the two Thai monks who had taken over from Ajahn Pabhakaro were guarding him pretty carefully, limiting the time visitors could see him. After several days in town, I got a ride with Ajahn Pabhakaro, whose parents had just left. When we arrived, only a caretaker was there; Luang Por and the monks had taken a trip to Ratburi, a couple of hours south. So we waited for most of the day, and they returned at dusk. Luang Por seemed pretty much the same as before. But as he sat and talked with a layman, at one point he just drifted off in mid-sentence, and it was too much effort for him to bring his attention back and continue talking. It was a little frightening to see.

Ajahn Pabhakaro and I sat alone with him for a while. His mind was clear but he was obviously exhausted. I asked him if he sometimes thought to leave his body behind and go where he might be more comfortable. "Where should I go?" he growled. I said that I didn't know, but I thought maybe he could be more comfortable without the burden of dragging his body around. He looked at me very fiercely and said, "You want me to die?" After that, I figured that he had his reasons for staying alive.

I went once more, with Ajahn Jagaro and Puriso, who were taking leave of him before going to Australia. We arrived in late morning, and he was having his second meal. He no longer ate out of his bowl with the others, but sat at a table for both meals, and the attendant monks wouldn't let anybody talk to him while he ate. When he finished and received us, he could just barely pay attention. There was nothing to discuss; it was like the two disciples were merely doing what was required in taking leave of him and asking for forgiveness, but he wasn't really the same man who had been their teacher all those years. I carried this impression with me for the next month and a half, figuring the end was near for him, but the next time I saw him he was better, not worse; and so it was to go, up and down, for several months. This was February of 1982. When I returned in April, Kesaree told me that he'd been worse for a while, he thought he was going to die and told them to take him back to Ubon because he didn't want to trouble the people in Samut Sakorn with his corpse. But they told him it would be an honor if he were to lay down his khandhas there, so he stayed, but didn't die, a trick he may have learned from his mother: on many occasions she thought she was dying and asked to see her coffin, and after she saw it she would always recover (except for one time).

The day before I left for Sri Lanka I was supposed to go with some lay people to see Luang Por again. We were to meet early and go there to offer food, but when I arrived at Mr. Manun's house, he said, "Luang Por's disappeared." He had picked up and gone somewhere and hadn't left a forwarding address. It was a disappointment not to be able to see him before leaving, but I was glad to see that he still had some mischief in him.

Next stop, Sri Lanka. Up to now my game plan had worked well, and I was in high spirits. I went to a meditation center that had been recommended to me, outside of Kandy on a hilltop above the tea fields. An idyllic location, but it was crowded, and it felt a little strange to be living with lay people again. After two weeks I took to the road, stopped to check out the British hill station of Newar Eliya, and ended up at a hermitage in Bandarawela. It was a sturdy place built out of stone and concrete by a European monk. There were only an English bhikkhu and a Japanese anagarika living there. It was quiet, the climate temperate, the food adequate though fiery—after each meal my eyes and nose would be watering and my stomach contracted from the chillies that were in everything. I had all day to meditate. It was just the kind of place I'd been looking for, and after a few days my meditation hit the skids and my game plan came unraveled. What to do? I didn't find the practice scene in Sri Lanka particularly energizing for various reasons. The Sangha didn't seem to have the cohesiveness that pulled you along with it through the ups and downs as it did in Thailand. Back in Thailand it was hot season. Somehow I didn't feel ready for going to Japan. What to do? I started fantasizing about getting a job in Thailand with one of the many refugee programs there. The worst it could be was stalling for time—I would still be in Asia while I decided where to go next.

So after a month in Sri Lanka I was back in Bangkok. It was a pleasant surprise to find the weather moderate. But something had happened while I was trying to practice the previous month. I found that as soon as I left the hermitage and hit the streets, I felt completely disoriented, I staggered around like a crazy man, unable to do things or make decisions. After two weeks in Bangkok I was pretty frazzled. If I had been willing to stay in Bangkok longer I probably would have gotten a job, but I'd had enough. I realized I hadn't come to Asia to work. In a somewhat desperate state of mind I decided to go back to Bung Wai for a tune-up, or maybe an overhaul.

But I've forgotten about Luang Por, haven't I?

He was still in Samut Sakorn, and I was able to get a ride out there when some Bung Wai monks came to Bangkok and wanted to go see him. To my relief, he was in better condition than he'd been in February. His physical condition was pretty delicate, but his mind was clear, he joked with us and even remembered people's names, which he had never been very good at. He asked me what I was going to do next. Not sure, I said. "Ajahn Not-Sure," he laughed. He asked me about my time in Ubon, which he hadn't done the last time I'd seen him. I said that it was good living in the wat again, but it wasn't easy, and I'd come to feel that anyone who could live like that deserves respect. "Varapanyo yorm laew," he said, which translates somewhere between "Varapanyo concedes" and "Varapanyo says uncle." I told him I'd visited Ajahn Jun, but hadn't stayed long because "Ajahn Jun was disturbing me." How was he disturbing you? "Dharma talks." Luang Por innocently asked, "What do you think, do the Dharma talks have some value?" I replied that I figured it was a good way of disciplining the majority of Thai monks, who otherwise wouldn't be likely to practice, but for someone like myself there was no point to it. "Lazy guy," he laughed. Then I told him I'd stayed in a cave at Tam Saeng Pet for a while and really liked it there. "What did you do in the cave?" he asked. I said that I'd done sitting and walking meditation—it seemed like a strange question, I don't know what else someone could do there. "You mean you didn't just sleep all the time? ... Varapanyo goes to stay in the cave, he sleeps night and day. He wakes up after dawn: 'Oh! Is it time for the meal?' So he runs up to the sala, eats his meal, then comes back to the cave to sleep again ... " Well, it was actually good to hear him talk like this again, it was a sign that he was feeling better.

Back to Ubon. The heat wasn't too bad that year. Just to be in the monastery was a great relief after Bangkok. I soon calmed down, and I realized that just by being there, without making any special great effort to practice, my mind was much clearer than it was when

I was on the outside. I was not so much a tourist or a retreatant this time, I'd really come seeking shelter, refuge, and it made a lot of sense to live like that. In one of his fortnightly talks, Ajahn Pasanno had said, "When you live in a simple environment, your mind can become uncomplicated." Amen. Many a time as I walked around the monastery, with no more concern other than to watch out for biting ants, I thought of what it would be like if I was "out there" with a million things competing for my attention. It was more than I wanted to deal with, and there didn't seem much reason to.

Unfortunately, in my hurry to leave Sri Lanka I had only gotten a two month visa for Thailand. When it expired I decided to go to Penang to get another three months and come right back to the wat.

Luang Por was back at Soi 81, I think for his monthly checkup at Samrong Hospital. Ajahn Pabhakaro and the two Thai monks were with him. All of a sudden he seemed to be the old Luang Por again. He couldn't have walked a 7 km pindapat, but he didn't have that feeling of fragility or being ill. His mind was extremely sharp. I hung around there with him a few evenings and there was a very relaxed, happy feeling. It was almost too good to be true. But the doctors had said he'd need six months, and it was now almost seven (late May, 1982). The monks had been controlling his diet and limiting visitors, and it seemed to have paid off. In the morning they let people bring food inside to Luang Por themselves, and afterwards would tell the people that he had to rest. But if I came later in the day they let me in. Luang Por was planning to go back to Ubon for his annual birthday celebration, perhaps to stay. A specially designed kuti was under construction, though it was originally supposed to be ready in April, then for his birthday, and now they were saying maybe for vassa (they didn't come close to that either). He asked me if I could drive. I said yes—maybe he'd forgotten how nervous he got with me behind the wheel in New York—and he said that someone was giving him a van, so we could take trips to visit the branch monasteries. He even started taking trips around Bangkok and nearby places to get in shape for it, and I started planning on being a chauffeur.

But as we all know by now, things are not certain in this world. When I came back from Penang not so many days later, he was

167

gone, back to Samut Sakorn. I bought a bus ticket for Ubon and figured I'd see him there. The day I was leaving I went by Soi 81 to visit Ajahn Pabhakaro, and while I was there a phone call came saying that Luang Por was coming back. We cleaned the kuti and waited, but I had to leave for the bus before he arrived.

The tour bus let me off right by the monastery at 6 AM. As soon as I stepped out of its air-conditioned splendor I was hit by hot humid air. It wasn't a nice reception, and I knew that if it was like this early in the morning, the days were going to be pretty miserable. Which they were for a while, which revived various dissatisfactions. I wrote to my friend in Surin to send me a cake with a file in it, but none came. I still looked forward to being Luang Por's driver, though.

A monk came from Bangkok and told us that Luang Por had been doing too much and his condition had gone down again. When he arrived in mid-June he was in pretty bad shape. It was all downhill from there. He was in a wheelchair most of the time, his voice was weak, memory and attention limited. For his birthday celebration, he walked into the sala with a few people assisting him and was barely able to do the ceremony of forgiveness. There was no Dharma talk. Ajahn Pasanno said later that it should have been obvious to everyone there that Luang Por was not the same man anymore; he looked like he was 90 years old.

When I'd see him, he would ask, "Aren't you going to Sri Lanka?" and I figured that past and present were all jumbled in his mind. But at other times when he was being wheeled around the monastery, people would come up to him and he'd remember who they were, where they came from, who their relatives were.

I think there was resentment among the Ubon people, who felt that Luang Por had been stolen away by people in Bangkok and returned in this sad condition. It's a touchy subject, and at the time I felt that the country bumkins just didn't understand the situation— indeed, the monks were poorly prepared for taking care of him and the lay people didn't show great consideration—but more recently in Bangkok I heard one of the lay supporters voice serious doubt about the way the matter was handled by the doctors involved, that perhaps the operation wasn't necessary after all, etc. One Western monk said he met a man who was a doctor who was grief-stricken over the whole thing and claimed that the Bangkok doctors had used Luang Por as a guinea pig for their new technology. The question will probably never be answered. Luang Por's condition was complicated by diabetic tendencies and several other things so it's doubtful that he would have had many more years of good health in any case.

I was staying at Bung Wai during this time and visiting Wat Bah Pong every week or 10 days. Each time I went I could see further deterioration. Ajahn Pabhakaro went to Bangkok at one point to consult with the doctors, and some of them flew up to Ubon. They were the King's doctors, the best available. They didn't really know what to make of Luang Por's condition, but they thought that maybe he had a brain tumor and suggested bringing him to Chulalongkorn Hospital for tests. At this point he was losing control of his bladder, couldn't walk more than a few steps, was having laughing and crying spells, and hardly ever speaking.

Back at Bung Wai the vassa had begun. There was a good schedule with many hours of group meditation, but in the heat it was often a struggle to keep hanging in there. At least there were cushioned mats to sit on, and we in the back row could use zafus or other such illegal things (this was another of my long-standing disputes with the stubbornness of the Thai monastic system—as a monk I was always sneaking in wads of cloth to sit on, or sitting on the rolled up end of my *sanghati*, the outer robe which is usually folded into a long narrow strip and worn over the shoulder; sometimes I would sit on my flashlight. Some sat on books. As we all know, raising the buttocks helps to straighten the back. But Thais prefer to sit slumped over rather than break with custom).

When my visa was coming to an end once more, I was undecided about what to do. I left for Bangkok when Luang Por went. When I saw him in Chulalongkorn Hospital, it was a real shock. He'd stopped talking and had the look of a dying man, who may know what's going on around him but doesn't take an interest anymore. At that point I was pretty sure that he wouldn't live more than a few months.

Still undecided about what to do, I skipped town for a few days and went to Wat Kow Chalak in Chonburi. Luang Por Put, a Wat Bah Pong monk, was there. He "confirmed" that Ajahn Kampoon, one of the senior monks at Wat Bah Pong who had recently left and was rumored to have died, was really gone. "It's true. He died of malaria. They cremated him in Bangkok." It wasn't until three years later that I found out Ajahn Kampoon is alive and kicking in southern Thailand—some lay people from Ubon, who'd also heard of his demise, came across him there, which gave them quite a start. Anyhow, after a few days of intense heat and swarms of thirsty mosquitoes, I decided that I'd had enough of the tropics for the time being and reconfirmed my flight to California.

I visited the King's suite in the hospital, where Luang Por was staying, a few more times, but usually I just prostrated to the door of his room and talked with Ajahn Pabhakaro and the nursing staff. When talking with Thai people in such situations (i.e. anywhere near monks or a monastery) it would inevitably come out that I'd been a monk, and they'd want to know why I'd disrobed. I would usually give everyone a different answer, but whatever the answer was, they'd most likely say how sorry they were that I disrobed. If they were lay people, I'd tell them that they didn't have to feel sorry because they could ordain in my place, "there's a seat open now." For which they'd always have a multitude of excuses: I'm too old, I'm too young, I've got to take care of my children, I've got to help my mother, etc.

The doctors had run all kinds of tests but found nothing new. There didn't seem to be anything to do for Luang Por but let him go back to Ubon and live out whatever time he had left. I was pretty certain it wouldn't be very long, and that I'd never see him again, though even if I were to somehow see him at some future time, the Luang Por I knew was gone forever, there would be no more teaching, no more laughs or insults. Well, that was seven years ago, and he's still hanging on. Between 1984 and 1986 I went to see him a few times, but it was hard to think of him as Luang Por, and there didn't seem to be any recognition on his part. In late '86 he'd gone through a couple of crises, and his immanent departure was predicted by both a monk who was famed for the accuracy of his predictions and a team of the Queen's doctors who said he had cancer. He was being spoon fed, could only move one hand and open one eye, yet he's continued on since then.

There's a story of Mulla Nasrudin in the teahouse, where some soldiers were recounting their exploits on the battlefield. After listening to their proud stories, Nasrudin spoke up. "Once in battle I cut off the leg of an enemy. Severed it straight through." Someone said to him, "Sir, you would have done better to have cut off his head." Nasrudin replied, "I'm afraid that would not have been possible. You see, somebody had already done that." That was how I was feeling about my time in the monasteries on this trip. It might seem heroic to some back home, but I didn't think I'd personally done anything special. However, I did feel that I'd been very fortunate to be able to return there and see things from the point of view of renunciation once more. The difficulties I encountered made me a little more tolerant of my imperfections, and I hoped that I might someday be able to extend that attitude to others—that was a major problem for me after I disrobed and was associating with lay practicers—though living in the wat made it very clear how different monks and lay people are. When lay people would come to visit or stay for a while, whether Thai or Western, their behavior always seemed pretty crude, and their worldly involvements and attachments were sometimes amusing and often left one feeling sorry for them. I suppose the monks may well have seen me like that, too. I often thought of Dogen's statements about the superiority of the monk's way of life. He even said that a monk who is stupid, breaks the precepts and has no wisdom is superior to a layman who keeps precepts and possesses insight, because only the monk has Buddha's enlightenment as the basis of his way of life, and that enlightenment is the same as, and manifests in, renunciation of the world. I might not buy that 100%, but it's very compelling when contemplated in the midst of monastic life rather than from an armchair. For those on the outside, such things are difficult to understand. After Buddha's enlightenment, He thought, "This truth which I have realized is profound, difficult for ordinary people to see," and after I returned home I felt that this applied to monastic life as well, as it was the practical manifestation of that truth. Yet as Suzuki Roshi said, when you're living in the monastery it's nothing special or strange; it's just the sensible way to live, and actually it's the lay people who seem strange when you see them and contemplate their funny clothes, their opinions, emotions, and worldly involvements.

VENERABLE FATHER

Two months after I left Thailand I went to the fall retreat at Barre, and was soon flooded by memories of Luang Por, dreams about him, strong emotions, etc., so after the retreat I started writing all this down as an offering to him and his disciples. I eventually started doing Vajrayana practice and began to feel somewhat distant from the whole Theravada scene, but I was also experiencing severe "culture shock" as I hadn't experienced after I disrobed. Western society and especially the U.S. seemed most psychotic and not a healthy place to live. I finally became very fond of Thailand. For years I'd always been puzzled when people told me how much they liked Thailand, but now it compared very favorably. I began to see the four years between disrobing and returning to Asia as a transition period. I didn't feel like either California or New York were places for me to settle. Some friends were talking about building retreat cabins in the Colorado mountains, but I was broke and it seemed like an impossibility for me. As time went by I longed to get back to Asia, and when I was finally ready to go, Thailand seemed like the choice for a number of reasons, and once in Thailand, Wat Bung Wai and the other Wat Bah Pong monasteries were the places I felt most at home in. Meanwhile Luang Por had survived. He gets the best possible care, and the doctors say that all his organs function well except for his brain. Wat Bah Pong has become a ghost town (ghost wat) with just a skeleton crew of monks to take care of things, but there haven't been the mass disrobings many of us expected. Monks have gone off on their own or to the many branch monasteries (over 60 now) and practice and teaching continue, with the Sangha in good harmony. New people keep on showing up at Wat Bung Wai to train and ordain, large numbers of farang come for short stays, and the legendary Varapanyo appears every so often, though he is no longer young. The Sangha flourishes in England, is growing in Australia, and has set up shop in New Zealand. Jack and I finally got our book of Luang Por's teachings published in the U.S. and it is proving the experts, who said it wouldn't sell, wrong. The story continues.

Afterword

Traveling through Thailand and England, visiting Ajahn Chah's monasteries as well as the homes of former monks, one thing comes through consistently, and that is the love, gratitude and high regard for Ajahn Chah of all those who spent a part of their lives under his guidance. From the simple remark, "Luang Por was good, wasn't he?" to the statement that "he was the most remarkable person I ever met ... and one of the greatest men Thailand has ever produced," it is quite obvious how he reached people and shaped their lives for the better.

When Ajahn Chah first went to the uninhabited forest of Nong Bah Pong some 40 years ago, I doubt he ever imagined that a worldwide network of monasteries would someday come into existence. Certainly the motley handful of Occidentals who found their way there in the late 1960's and early 1970's weren't thinking of such things. Yet it has all developed quite naturally. There have been growing pains, personality clashes, at times sharp differences of opinion, but the monasteries have preserved and transmitted traditional Buddhist practice, offering refuge and a way towards liberation for vast numbers of people.

Venerable Ajahn Jagaro once remarked that Ajahn Chah was a

teacher you could not only respect, but also love. Even after so many years it remains clear what a very skillful and caring teacher he was. Perhaps with the passage of time, with the deepening of various individuals' experience, or simply the opportunity to reflect, what Luang Por was doing with us, how capable and thorough he was, how completely he gave of himself, and how vast and exalted was his wisdom will become even clearer. Listening to people's praises of him, I never felt that they were trying to canonize him or build him up into something he wasn't. On the contrary, people just seemed to be speaking matter-of-factly about what it was like to be his disciple, and yet I'm sure we would all agree that we still couldn't really say who he was. In the end we can just refer to him as Luang Por, and that name will always evoke the magical experience of having known him.

September, 1994

GLOSSARY

Ajahn (Th.) (P. - *Acariya*) - teacher.

Ajahn Mun - Probably the most well-known of the Thai forest masters, he was the teacher of many of the masters of Ajahn Chah's generation. He died in 1949.

Amper (Th.)- township.

Anagarika (P.)- "homeless one," usually referring to a layman keeping the Eight Precepts (refraining from taking life, stealing, sex, lying, intoxicants, food in the afternoon, adornments and entertainments, and soft beds).

Bhikkhu (P.) -a fully-ordained Buddhist monk.

Dharma (Skt.)- the Buddha's teaching; religious teaching; reality; natural truth.

Devadatta - the Buddha's cousin who became jealous of him and created a schism of the Sangha, and eventually attempted to kill him.

Eightfold Path - the Buddha's way to liberation: Right View, Right Intention, Right Speech, Right Action, Right Livelihood, Right Effort, Right Mindfulness, Right Meditation.

Farang (Th.) - A Westerner.

Four Noble Truths - The truths of suffering (P. dukkha), its cause, its cessation, and the Eightfold Path leading to cessation.

Isan (Th.) - The northeast of Thailand

Jhana (P.) - meditative absorption.

Kanoy (L.) - a polite exclamation used at the beginning or end of a sentence.

Kathina (P.) (Th. - *Katin*) - ceremony of offering robe material to the Sangha in the month following the 3 month rains residence.

Krup (Th.) - "yes", also can be added at the end of a sentence for politeness.

Mahanikaya (P.) - one of the two sects of the Thai monastic order, older and much larger than the reformist Dhammayut (P. Dhammayuttikanikaya).

Metta (P.) - loving-kindness.

Pah Bah (Th.)- similar to a Kathina ceremony, but not as formal, and it can be done at any time of the year.

Parajika (P.) - offenses for which one is expelled from the Order - killing a human being, stealing, sexual intercourse, falsely claiming supramundane attainments.

Parivasa (P.) -process of penance and purification for monks committing Sanghadisesa offences.

Patimokkha (P.)- the 227 basic rules of a bhikkhu. Infractions are confessed fortnightly and the rules recited in Pali in a formal gathering, also called the Uposatha ceremony.

Sabai (Th.) - well, happy, comfortable.

Sakah (Th.) - branch (monastery).

Sala (Th.) - the main meeting/meditation hall in a monastery.

Samanera (P.) (Th. - nen)- novice.

Sangha - the community of Buddhist practicers. In Thailand it usually refers to the monastic community.

Sanghadisesa (P.) - a class of heavy offenses which "entail initial and final meeting of the Sangha." There are thirteen offenses in this class.

Sangharaja (P.) - the head of the entire Thai monastic order. There are several Somdet (Th.) next in command.

Sila (P.) - moral conduct, precepts.

Soi (Th.) - side streets. Most major city roads have numbered soi.

Tam wat (Th.)- chanting; sometimes specifically meaning a ceremony of paying respect to teachers and asking forgiveness for transgressions of body, speech, and mind.

Three characteristics - impermanence, unsatisfactoriness, not-self.

Tudong (Th.) (P.- *dhutanga*) - 13 ascetic practices allowed to monks; commonly refers to travelling on foot, living in the open. Ajahn Chah would encourage his monks to spend at least some time on extended periods of tudong, traveling on foot through forested areas.

Vinaya (P.)- the collection of scriptures elucidating the monastic discipline; the monastic discipline.

Wai (Th.)- joining the palms in greeting or respect.

Wun Pra (Th.) - lunar observance day, on the half, full, and new moons.